ALL-TERRAIN PUSHCHAIR WALKS
West Yorkshire

Rebecca Chippindale and Rebecca Terry

Published by Sigma Leisure – an imprint of
Sigma Press, Stobart House, Pontyclerc, Penybanc Road, Ammanford,
Carmarthenshire SA18 3HP.

British Library Cataloguing in Publication Data
A CIP record for this book is available from the British Library.

ISBN: 978-1-85058-881-8

Typesetting and Design by: Sigma Press,

Cover photograph: Suprise View, Chevin
Elsdon)

Maps and graphics: Rebecca Terry

Photographs: Rebecca Terry and Phillip E

Printed by: Berforts Group Ltd, Stevenage

Disclaimer: the information in this book is given in good faith and is
believed to be correct at the time of publication. No responsibility is
accepted by either the author or publisher for errors or omissions, or for
any loss or injury howsoever caused. Only you can judge your own
fitness, competence and experience. Do not rely solely on sketch maps
for navigation; we strongly recommend the use of appropriate Ordnance
Survey (or equivalent) maps.

Preface

Why should having a baby get in the way of your enjoyment of walking? This book makes it easy for parents and grandparents to set off with an all-terrain pushchair (ATP) to enjoy some of the best walking in West Yorkshire.

All the walks are designed to keep your little one happy – not only with the variety of routes (we chose woodland, moorland, canals, parks, walks with a train journey in the middle …) but, where possible, fitting in stops for baby-changing, duck feeding or ice-cream eating! You can simply choose the terrain to suit the mood of you and your child(ren) – from a light stroll on an easy path to some more strenuous off-roading. Whichever you choose, you can be safe in the knowledge that each walk has already been done with an ATP and is therefore definitely do-able.

We have put at-a-glance symbols at the top of each walk so you can see without having to read the whole walk how long it will take, what footwear you need, whether or not there are any steep hills, if there are picnic tables or even if there is a child-friendly pub along the way! There are a whole host of other hints to make each trip as easy and fun as possible, so whichever walk you do, you can know before you go!

There is also the added bonus of our 'in the area' section. This gives you one or two ideas for other activities near the walk you choose. So you can set off for the whole day, doing a walk in the morning and then, for example visiting an urban farm or soft play centre in the afternoon (even via a picnic spot en-route). Most of these suggestions have addresses and phone numbers so you can call ahead for opening times and prices.

We really hope you enjoy these walks as much as we did with our babies Jamie and Molly. What a perfect way to both keep fit and introduce your child to some beautiful sights in West Yorkshire. Happy pram-pushing!

Rebecca Chippindale and Rebecca Terry

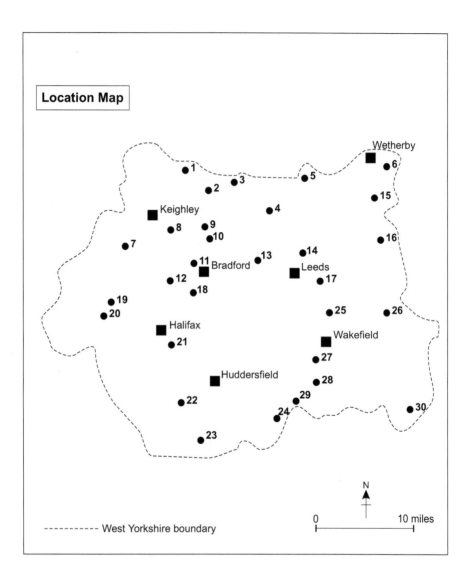

Location Map

Wetherby

1
3
2
5
6
15
4
Keighley
8
9
10
16
7
13
14
11 Bradford
Leeds
12
17
18
19
25
26
20
Halifax
21
Wakefield
27
Huddersfield
28
22
29
24
30
23

N

0   10 miles

- - - - - - - - - West Yorkshire boundary

Contents

Introduction

This book contains thirty pushchair-friendly walks in West York-shire. The majority of walks are circular routes and many have options for shortening or lengthening to suit. Walks range from 1 to 5 miles in length, giving plenty of choice for both leisurely strollers and experienced ramblers. West Yorkshire has a rich and diverse landscape and these walks cover some of the best walking the region has to offer.

Routes and Grades

As mentioned in the preface, we have made this book as easy to follow as possible. Our at-a-glance key tells you all you need to know about the walk ahead – from distance, terrain and physical effort required to facilities, car parking and any hidden costs, so there won't be any nasty surprises when you get there. You can see whether or not the walk is do-able with just one person or whether two people are required.

Always allow more time than recommended. The times given are approximate and based on an average walking speed of two miles per hour. However, everyone walks at a different pace and the times given don't make allowances for picnics and other breaks.

We have kept the maps as simple, yet informative as possible allowing for basic route finding when used in conjunction with the route directions. There is a start point marked on each map and numbers which refer to instructions within the walk text. We would always recommend taking Ordnance Survey Explorer map(s) with you. Each walk has details of the map required and a grid reference for the start point.

Advice for First-Time Buyers

Here are a few helpful tips when buying an All-Terrain Pushchair:

It is very important to check that your child is old enough to be safe in an All-Terrain Pushchair (ATP). Many can be used from birth upwards, but some cannot. Very young babies should not be bumped or shaken around too much, so seek advice from manufacturers and choose your routes extremely carefully in the beginning. We wouldn't recommend any walks other than our lowest grading for children under 3 months.

Make sure it has pneumatic tyres as these, as well as good suspension, provide a lot of cushioning over the rough terrain.

Check the pram is as lightweight as possible – an aluminium frame is usually the best.

Go for a long wheel base rather than a short wheel base as this provides extra stability. Also, a fixed front wheel is better if you are doing a lot of off-roading – much better than a lockable swivel wheel.

Check it folds easily and will fit both in your car and go though your front door! Quick-release wheels are always good if your car boot isn't that big.

Accessories: If not already included in the price, be sure to purchase a rain cover and a good quality footmuff (preferably with wind protection). Sun shades which cover the whole front of the ATP are now available in a mesh material which your child can see

Single and Double All-Terrain Pushchairs from the 'Mountain Buggy' range. *Reproduced by permission of Chariots All-Terrain Pushchairs* www.pushchairs.co.uk

through and though quite pricey, are much better than faffing around with a parasol.

It is also worth checking if the pram comes with a small puncture repair kit and pump – and if not, buy one. You know you will get a puncture if you don't take one along!

Another item we have found very useful is a pram leash. This is simply a strap or piece of rope attached to the ATP handle with a loop at the other end to put your hand through. This provides added security when you are on slippery ground or going downhill.

Shop around. Both ATPs on the front cover were second-hand buys from the internet. It is always worth looking in the shops first and then checking the net for the same pram at a better price – either new or used.

A Useful Checklist before Leaving the House

For baby

h   Pram with rain cover, sun cover, footmuff and puncture repair kit.

h   Picnic. Obviously sandwiches are great if your baby is eating on his/her own, but if not, go for yoghurts, fruit pots, anything easy to open, and don't forget the spoon. A spare carrier bag is useful to bundle up all the debris to take home or dispose of afterwards.

h   Snacks to keep your little treasure jollied along. If your child is old enough, try small boxes of raisins as they take ages to eat!

h   Water/juice.

h   Milk – if you are not breastfeeding, we find the best thing is to take a couple of ready-made cartons to just pour into the bottle as needed. If your baby has heated milk, make it extra hot before you go, wrap it in foil or muslin and by the time you need it, it should be about right!

h   A spare set of clothes in case of food or nappy accidents! It is a good idea to have a few layers of clothes rather than one chunky item as they can be put on/peeled off to suit. Don't forget that although you may be hot from the uphill pushing, your baby has been sat still. Keep checking to make sure he/she isn't getting too cold.

h We found one of the best buys was an all-in-one fleece for baby. Many have foot and hand holes which fold over at the ends to serve as gloves. Worn over an all in one babygrow, these can be very comfortable.

h A couple of nappies/wipes/nappy bags.

h Shoes for when he/she wants to get out of the pram.

For you

h Appropriate shoes and coat etc. Keep a cagoule in the bottom of the pram for emergencies.

h Food and drink; it's so easy to forget your own lunch when you are packing the bags!

h A mobile phone.

h Small first aid kit.

h The ATP book, so you will know where you're going!

The Countryside Code

h Respect – Protect – Enjoy.

h Do not drop litter. Use a bin or take it home.

h Do not stray from public footpaths or bridleways (unless on access land).

h Do not pick any plants.

h Make no unnecessary noise.

h Keep dogs on a lead near livestock and under close control at all other times.

h Leave gates as you find them.

h Use gates or stiles to cross fences, hedges or walls.

h Do not touch livestock, crops or farm machinery.

h   Keep the natural water supply clean.

h   Walk in single file and on the right-hand side of roads.

h   Do not cross railway lines except by bridges.

h   Guard against the risk of fire.

For information on new access rights, visit www.countrysideaccess.gov.uk or telephone 0845 100 3298.

West Yorkshire

The terrain of Yorkshire is so varied that there's a walk to suit everyone. West Yorkshire is no different. From open moorland to the smaller urban, industrial pockets of the region, we hope both newcomers to the area, as well as long-term residents will be surprised by the richness and diversity of this area.

Each walk has an introductory section giving you some interesting background about the area. We have also included an 'in the area' section. This gives details of other ways to entertain your kids and yourself while you are there.

Circular route.

There and back. Route is non-circular.

Easy route with very few hills.

Moderate exertion. Some gentle ascents and descents.

Hard going. Route incorporates some steep inclines.

Easy terrain, trainers suitable.

Muddy and wet. Wellington boots or hiking boots are required.

Rough terrain. Rocky and uneven ground, hiking boots recommended.

Stile.

Icecream van on route!

Tea shop.

Pub/Hotel.

Picnic table.

Children's playground.

Ducks!

Toilets.

Solo. Walk can be accomplished alone.

At least two people required to complete walk. Pushchair may need to be lifted over obstacles.

Money required for parking, entrance fee or rail fare.

Walk 1: White Wells – Darwin Gardens, Ilkley

Allow: *1 hour 15 minutes (or 45 minutes)*

This varied walk passes through Ilkley moor to White Wells Spa, The Tarn and the Darwin Gardens Millennium Green. The first part of the walk, which can be left out, goes over open moorland and will challenge your offroad ability! An all-terrain pushchair is definitely required for this 30-minute section. However, those who fancy an easy 45-minute stroll or who have four-wheel pushchairs can enjoy a walk around The Tarn and the gardens (see note at end of walk description).

Ilkley is a moorland town on the edge of the Yorkshire Dales. It owes much of its present form to the building and popularity of the spa baths on the edge of Ilkley moor, which brought hotels and wealth into the area. White Wells Spa dates back to 1756 and is fed by three springs noted for the pureness of their water. It was the first hydropathic spa for the 'cold water cure' and was used by Charles Darwin in 1859. It is now run as a museum and tea shop.

Map: Ordnance Survey 1:25000 Explorer 297 – grid reference 115469

Distance: 1½ miles

Getting there: Park in the White Wells free car park on Wells Road.

Go up the hill past the sign for White Wells Spa cottage (open weekends for snacks and information). As you go up the hill the track goes over a beck at Spout Falls.

> There are a number of wooden benches along this track from which you can appreciate the spectacular views over Ilkley and lower Wharfedale. The large stone house over the road from the car park is Wells House, a former hydropathic establishment designed by Cuthbert Brodrick. This was, until recently, Bradford and Ilkley community college but is now a residential development.

White Wells Spa, Ilkley Moor

1. After approximately 15 minutes you will reach White Wells cottage where there are picnic tables and toilets. Go past the front of the cottage, down a few small steps and along to a large pond. There are benches around the pond if you fancy stopping for a break.

   Just before you get to the pond there is a path off to the left. Go along this footpath and follow it down the hill ignoring any paths off to the left and right. This track is quite rocky in places and has a number of steps but, as you are travelling down the hill, it is relatively easy to negotiate. However, be careful in wet weather as this path can become muddy and slippery.

2. The track leads you down to a tarmac footpath, turn right here towards The Tarn. This footpath circles the lake so you can go either direction. There are benches all the way round and a covered seating area, making this a lovely place to stop for a while.

   Once you have been around the lake go back down the tarmac

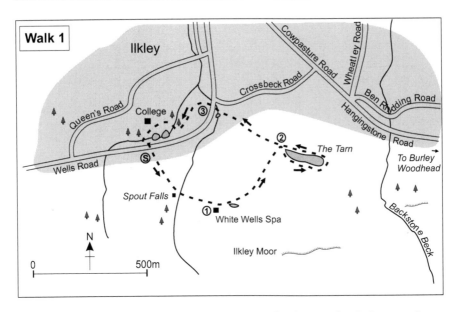

path towards Ilkley. When you reach the end of the track go through the kissing gate and down towards Wells road.

At the kissing gate there is a path that goes back up onto the moor. If you have time you can go up to a paddling pool and to another covered seating area with great views. In addition, on the right here is Hillside Court where Charles Darwin once resided.

When you get to the road turn left and go through the wooden gate next to the cattle grid. Cross the road and enter the car park of Darwin Gardens Millennium Green. At the far side of the car park there is a sign explaining the layout of the gardens. There are also picnic tables here.

3. On the left of the car park you will see a slab carved with the image of Charles Darwin. Take the path to the left of this, which leads you to the millennium maze.

This maze has 1000 stone slabs to represent each year of the millennium and each of these is dedicated to a person or institution.

As you leave the maze turn left, ignore the first track to the left, and cross the wooden footbridge ahead of you. Immediately after the footbridge take the left fork of the track which takes you to a road. Turn right here and go through the kissing gate at the side of the cattle grid.

Follow the road around to the left ignoring the public footpath to the right. This road takes you past the front of Wells House and there is a pond and garden area on the left. Turn left up a small bridged walkway over the garden. Go through the kissing gate and cross the road into White Wells car park.

N.B. If you wish to do the easier shortened version of this walk turn right onto Wells Road from the car park instead of heading up the track to White Wells Spa. Walk down the road until you reach the cattle grid. Go through the kissing gate and turn right immediately up a short track. At the top of this track is another kissing gate, go through this and head up the tarmac path to The Tarn. Once at The Tarn follow the rest of the walk from section 2.

In the area

Ilkley is a lovely Yorkshire town and definitely worth a visit. It has plenty of tea shops but top of the list is **Betty's Café and tea rooms**. Betty's has a wide selection of tea and cakes and also a large teapot collection on display! They also have high chairs and baby changing facilities.

At the bottom of town near the River Wharfe there is a lovely **park with a children's play area** and also the **open-air lido** for cooling down in those hot summer months! This is the only open air pool in West Yorkshire and is open between spring bank holiday and September. N.B. The outdoor pool is not heated! Telephone 01943 600 453.

Walk 2: Burley-in-Wharfedale to Menston

Allow: *1 hour 30 minutes*

Enjoy this scenic walk in the Wharfe Valley, which incorporates a three-minute train journey at the beginning. You pass through farmland, some rather nice houses and eventually the village of Menston, which has a lovely big park. Why not stop off at the lovely delicatessen, Solo, and take your lunch to the park if it's a nice day? Failing that, there are a couple of pubs in the village worth a visit. I must mention also, that there is a stile on this walk, which means two people are required for a bit of lifting! And here's a bit of trivia for you: Eric Mowbray Knight (1897-1943), author of 'Lassie Come Home', was born in Menston.

Map: Ordnance Survey 1:25000 Explorer 297 – grid reference 174441

Distance: 2½ miles

Getting there: Get to Menston Railway station and hop on the Ilkley train. Get off the train at the next stop which is Burley-in-Wharfedale (this should take about three minutes).

Follow the 'Way Out' sign and turn left. You will pass houses on your right and the train track will be (not visible) on your left.

1. After about 30 minutes you will come to a large farmyard. Head towards the top left of the farm, where you should see a gate and a stile. Go through the gate and follow the path downwards. The track soon gets a bit narrow and stony, but is fine. After another few minutes, you come to another stile, this time without a gate at the side. Here you will need two people to get your pram over.

   Keep straight on this narrow path, which eventually brings you out onto Bleach Mill Lane. Turn right up Bleach Mill Lane, following signs for Dalesway Link, Leeds and Ebor Way.

Bleach Mill Lane, Menston

Incidentally, free-range eggs are often for sale at this farm. Just knock on the door and ask. Tea, coffee and cakes are also available at weekends.

2. When you get to the end of Bleach Mill Lane (it should take about twenty minutes), turn left and head into the village of Menston. Keep going almost to the end of the village, where you will see a lovely park, just at the top of Farnley Road.

3. If you want to head straight back to Menston train station, turn left down Farnley Road and go straight to the bottom. Turn left onto Station Road and soon you will see the train station on your right.

In the area

There is a **lovely big park** in the village of Menston with children's play areas.

St Leonard's Farm Park is just a few miles away on the A6038 to Bradford (Chapel Lane, Esholt, Bradford, BD17 7RB). There are

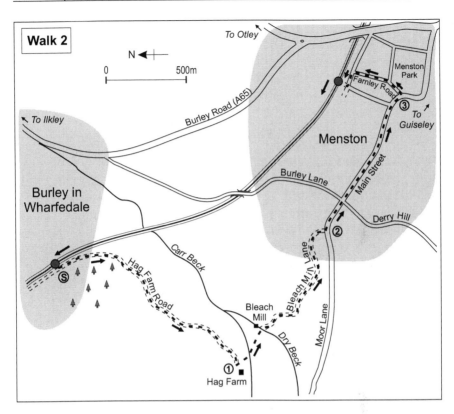

plenty of animals to see as well as pony and tractor rides, toddler trikes and electric ride-on tractors. For more information, check out the website www.stleonardsfarm.com or telephone 01274 598 795.

The **Hare & Hounds Pub** is just round the corner, with a **Wacky Warehouse** attached.

Or if you fancy fish & chips, then the world-famous **Harry Ramsden's** is in neighbouring Guiseley.

Walk 3: Danefield, Chevin Forest Park, Otley

Allow: *1 hour*

The Chevin Forest Park is popular with locals, and rightly so, as it is perfect for a tranquil walk any season of the year. However, the sandy paths can become very muddy during wet weather so wear appropriate footwear. The broad paths make this walk perfect for group outings so take your ATP friends along and catch up on the gossip on route! There are many paths through the forest (we have chosen just one possible route), allowing you to extend or shorten your walk as desired. In addition to sheltered walking within the forest, this walk also rewards you with spectacular views across lower Wharfedale.

Map: Ordnance Survey 1:25000 Explorer 297 – grid reference 215443

Distance: 2¼ miles

Getting there: When travelling from Otley, on the East Chevin road, you will see a sign for the Chevin Forest Park, Danefield gate. Park in the first car park on the left after this sign. At the entrance to this car park there is a footpath sign for Ebor Way and Dales Way link.

Walk through the gate at the far end of the car park and immediately turn left. A sign welcomes you to the Chevin Forest Park, Shawfield area. Follow the large central path which is signposted as a public bridleway, Dales Way link.

Soon you cross a bridge over a small stream and, ignoring the track to the left, continue up a short ascent until you come to a junction. Turn right up the public bridleway.

> Look out for the wooden carving of a girl holding a leaf. This is one of at least four sculptures within the park, see if you can spot them all as you go round.

Go up the hill and follow the path round along the border of the conifer forest. You pass a clearing on the left-hand side within which

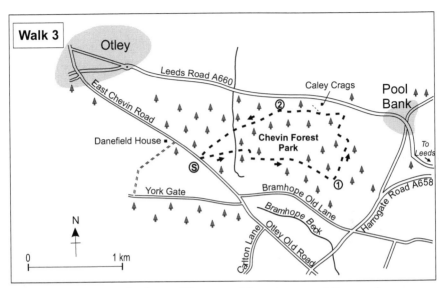

there is a triangulation pillar marking 242m. After a few more minutes you will come to a second clearing at which there is a junction in the path. Ignore all turnings on both sides and continue along the same bridleway.

> The path is now bordered with gorse bushes and on a warm spring day they brighten the walk with rich yellow flowers which release a wonderful coconut perfume.

1. After about five minutes you arrive at a T-junction, turn left. There are beech trees to your right which form the older part of the forest. Go down the hill and as the forest begins to open out you will come to a crossroads. Turn left along the Dales Way link.

   After a couple of minutes take the first turning on the right. Head down the hill until you arrive at a gate and bare left here. Another wooden carving can be found at this point.

   At the next fork in the path, turn left along the Ebor Way. The path becomes uneven for a short distance, so watch your step.

   > The path to the right takes you to the base of Caley Boulders - a popular area for local climbers.

2. After a short steep hill you will arrive at a great picnic spot with spectacular views over lower Wharfedale.

Chevin Forest Park

To the right you can make out the rocky crag of Almscliffe. Below is the town of Otley and in the distance on a clear day you may be able to see as far as Simon's Seat. Immediately below you, are lots of large boulders. Be careful that you don't throw sticks or kick stones over the edge here as they are likely to hit the climbers below!

Continue along the path ignoring turnings to the left and right. Cross the wooden footbridge and head up the hill following the path as it narrows. Ahead you should be able to see the car park. To the right there is a large grassy clearing with picnic tables at the forest edge. This makes an excellent place to stop for a snack before your journey home.

In the area

Otley is a pleasant market town with shops and tea shops for the adults. In addition there is **Play Days**, a soft play zone for older toddlers. Call for opening times (01943 468544).

Just up the road from the Chevin Forest Park, in Guiseley, is the world-famous **Harry Ramsden's** fish and chip shop.

Walk 4: Paul's Pond and Golden Acre Park, Leeds

Allow: *1 hour or 1 hour 40 minutes*

The beauty of this walk is that you can decide how far you want to go when you get there (as we all know, babies can be happy at the start of a walk ...). The walk just around Paul's Pond takes about an hour. If you incorporate the Lakeside or Woodland Walk, add on another forty minutes or so. If you do not have an all-terrain pushchair, the park option is probably the best.

Golden Acre Park first opened in 1932 and contained many amusements including a boating lake and miniature railway. The park was not a success and was closed in 1938. Leeds City Council reopened the park in 1945 and it now consists of 137 acres (55 hectares) containing botanical gardens, lakes and woodland. The café in the park has all baby facilities including high chairs, changing unit and they are happy to heat up food.

Map: Ordnance Survey 1:25000 Explorer 297 – grid reference 266417

Distance: 1½ or 2½ miles

Getting there: Park in the main car park off A660 Otley Road.

Follow the path downhill, with the fence on your right.

1. Cross over the green bridge and follow the wooden walkway through the trees. At the end of the wooden path turn right on to a dirt path. Keep straight on this path, ignoring any smaller paths. Soon you will get to a little wooden bridge over a stream. Cross over the bridge and keep to the path with the stream on the left-hand side.

   After another five minutes or so, you will come to a junction with a tree in the middle. Go left here, crossing over the stream again and then take your next right up a very small hill, where you will come to Paul's Pond.

The footbridge on route to Paul's Pond

2. Follow the path all the way around with the pond on your right. The walk around the pond should take about fifteen to twenty minutes.

When you have walked around the pond, go back down the small track and turn left. Keep straight on this track, until you can see a large steel gate in front of you. Walk past the gate so it's on your left and keep to this track (don't take the path which leads directly away from the gate).

After about ten minutes, you should arrive back at the small wooden bridge, which you crossed earlier. Cross the bridge and follow the path back the way you came. Eventually you will get to the wooden track again. Turn left onto the track and follow it back, over the green bridge.

Now you can either head back to the car park or extend the walk around Golden Acre Park.

3. If you want to go around the park, turn right after the green bridge and follow the path under the stone bridge. Then either follow the signposts for Woodland Walk or Lakeside Walk.

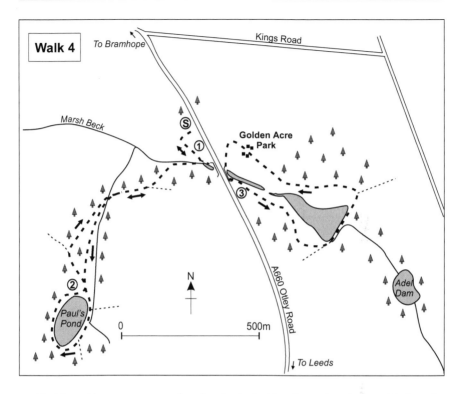

Both paths pass some lovely picnic tables in a clearing and lots of ducks to feed.

Incidentally, the Woodland and Lakeside Walks pass the park café on the way back.

In the area

Meanwood Valley Urban Farm is a good one for little children. They can see how a farm operates and see all the different animals. There is a picnic area and café as well as an organic market garden with some produce for sale. Often there are special child-orientated events held at the farm too. You do have to pay to get in, but for more information, call: 0113 262 9759. The address is: Sugarwell Road, Meanwood, Leeds LS7 2QG.

Walk 5: Harewood House, Harewood, Leeds

Allow: *2 hours 30 minutes*

This is a great walk, which takes in a mixture of easy bridle paths and rough terrain. There is plenty to see on route as you pass through farmland, fields and woodland. As it actually skirts round the estate, you do not have to pay to go in. The Queen's cousin, the Earl of Harewood, lives here, so you may even bump into royalty along the way.

If you decide to pay to see more of Harewood House estate, there's lots to see including a bird garden, boat trips across the lake and even an adventure playground. Inside Harewood House there is a huge art collection, impressive staterooms and a below-stairs exhibition. For more information about what's on at Harewood, go to www.harewood.org or telephone 0113 218 1010.

Map: Ordnance Survey 1:25000 Explorer 297 – grid reference 321449

Distance: 5 miles

Getting there: Harewood is mid-way between Leeds and Harrogate, on the A61.

Go through the main entrance under the arch and turn right, following the way out sign. You will pass Moor house on your right. Continue on this path for about five minutes and go through what looks like wrought iron railings. Turn left through the railings.

After about ten minutes, you will come to a cattle grid. Just on the left before the cattle grid is a path up to a church. There is a gate at the side of the cattle grid for ease. Go through the gate and continue straight ahead.

On your right are lovely views of lower Wharfedale.

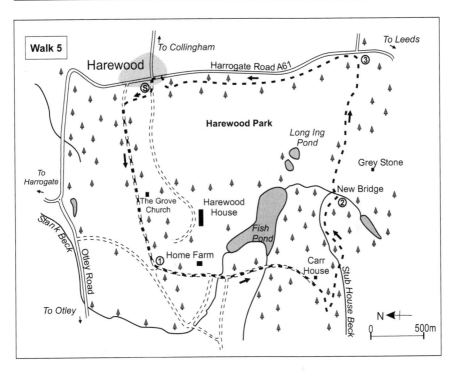

1. In five minutes or so, there is a triangle of grass. Bear left here, heading towards the sign, which says 'Private Road'.

   Keep your eyes peeled here, as there are often stags in this field.

   Shortly after, you will come to another cattle grid and gate. Continue straight over to Home Farm and Harewood Yard.

   Harewood Yard is an 18th-century farm complex in the middle of being converted for use as offices.

   Head straight on through the gate and up the hill over the beck. At the top of the hill, there is a fork in the road, take the right-hand turning (the public footpath). After a couple of minutes, you will come to a gate. Go through this and follow the footpath, which veers to the right.

   After a short while, you will see Carr House and a few cottages. Take the path to the right of Carr House, which takes you through

New Bridge

some woodland (this path becomes quite rugged and involves a bit of effort). Soon, there is a T-junction. Go right at the T-junction, following the public bridleway. After about a five-minute push uphill, you come to another T-junction – go left here.

After a few minutes, you should be able to see Harewood House poking through the trees on the left (the terrain gets much easier here).

Soon you will pass over Stubb House Beck. Turn left once you are over the beck. In about ten minutes or so, there's another triangle of grass where you turn left again.

Just ahead to the right, you can see a beautiful waterfall through the trees.

2. Soon you will come to a stone bridge – cross over the bridge and go through the gate ahead, following the path through the fields.

Here's a great place to see Harewood House from a distance on your left. Nan Pie wood is on your left a little further up, and there is a rock on your right called Grey Stone.

3. After about twenty minutes on this path, go through a large gate, where you will see the main road ahead. Turn left on to the Wallside Permissive Path (this is a very sensitive wildlife area, so please respect the environment).

After about half an hour on this path, you will see a big gate with a no entry sign. Turn right here and follow the path until you get to a wooden gate, with a ramshackle cottage to the left of it. Go through the gate, which takes you onto the main roadside (there is a pavement here). Gateways School is right in front of you.

Turn left and, within a minute, you will be at the entrance of Harewood House again, where the walk began.

In the area

As mentioned at the beginning of the walk, **Harewood House** itself is pretty impressive with lots to keep both young children and yourself entertained.

Time Machine, www.childrenstimemachine.co.uk, telephone 01423 816111, is an indoor adventure play and party centre in nearby Harrogate. There are soft play areas to suite all ages from babies to 10 years. It is open seven days a week and has a café with a separate microwave for use by parents to heat up baby food, bottes etc. There are also toilets with baby changing facilities.

Walk 6: River Wharfe, Boston Spa

Allow: 1 hour or 1 hour 45 minutes

A nice and easy, relaxing walk along the banks of the River Wharfe. This walk is perfect for a weekend stroll and, if the weather is good, why not take a picnic? The dirt paths are, for the most part, flat and easy to negotiate even with a four wheeler.

The walk passes along both the river bank and the woodland alongside it. Stop and have a look at the bridge built in 1770 and look out for herons, kingfishers and other wildlife. You will also walk through the old spa town of Boston Spa. The spa was discovered in 1744 and hot and cold water bath houses were built shortly after. The elegant Georgian architecture is all that remains to remind us of these prosperous days.

Map: Ordnance Survey 1:25000 Explorer 289 – grid reference 431456

Distance: 2 miles or 3½ miles

Getting there: Park in Boston Spa public car park, which is next to the library, on Bridge Road. There are public toilets here but no baby changing facilities.

Turn left on to Bridge Road and walk down towards the bridge. Cross the road and take the footpath signposted as riverside path, Ebor Way, just before the bridge. You will pass Hawthorn Cottage on your left and at a junction in the path, turn left towards the bridge. Go under the bridge and follow the path along the riverside.

There are picnic tables on the left immediately after the bridge.

1. You will soon come to a fork in the path at which point you should be able to see the weir through the trees. Go left here and at the next junction go straight on along the path to Deepdale. You will go up a series of small wooden steps and then the path levels out.

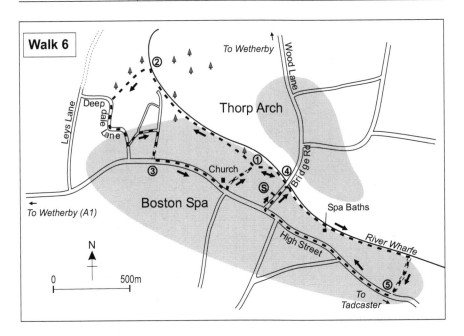

This path follows alongside fields and meadows to your left and a steep wooded river bank on your right.

2. After 20 minutes you will come to a short downhill section and a junction in the path. Take the path to the left and not the one that continues down the hill to the river. This path brings you to a very quiet country lane, turn left and walk along the road.

Follow the road as it bends, passing Deepdale House on your left and turn down the first road on the left, West Avenue. Take the next right down West Dale and at the end of this road turn right on to West End. This is a no through road but at the end there is a cycle path, which takes you up to the main road (High Street).

On your right there is a children's play area.

3. Turn left and walk along the road for about 5 minutes, which takes you back towards Boston Spa, until you come to St Mary's Church on the left. Take the bridleway immediately after the church down Holgate Lane. As you go down the path it heads

Bridge over the River Wharfe, Boston Spa

down in to woodland. You will come back to a junction you passed earlier (marker 1 on map) next to the weir. Turn right and follow the path back to the bridge.

4. You now have a choice. If you are ready to stop you can turn right up the path after the bridge and head up Bridge Road to the car park.

    If you want to extend your walk, continue along the riverside path. This path runs alongside the river for approximately 20 minutes. You will pass the Spa Baths and Wharfedale Hall. Shortly after Wharfedale Hall you come to a small junction in the path, follow the main path which curves round to the right. A narrow footpath does continue along the river bank but it is not suitable for pushchairs.

5. The dirt path, Wharfeside, soon becomes a gravel track. It passes between a number of houses and after 5 minutes brings you to a main road. Turn right here and follow the road (High Street) back into Boston Spa.

There are some very impressive examples of Georgian architecture along this road which were built when the town was a prosperous spa town.

After 15 minutes you will be back in Boston Spa. Turn right down Bridge Road to get back to the car park.

In the area

Boston Spa has a number of small shops including **Mother Goose** children's clothes shop. There are also some restaurants and a pub, the **Crown Hotel**.

The historic town of **Wetherby** is just 4 miles away, with shops, teashops and some more lovely riverside walks.

Walk 7: Brontë Bridge, Howarth

Allow: *1 hour 30 minutes*

The Brontë sisters lived in the parsonage in Haworth where their father was the church curate. The Brontë Way, as its name suggests, is a path that was often walked by the literary trio in their search for writing inspiration. This wonderful footpath passes through the South Pennine Moors and takes you to the beauty spots of Brontë Bridge and the Brontë Falls. Although it requires some effort to reach the bridge, it's a great place for a picnic and to bathe your feet in the stream on a hot summer's day. Those who are unsure about taking the pushchair over a rocky path should take a papoose instead.

Map: Ordnance Survey 1:25000 Outdoor Leisure 21 – grid reference 016365

Distance: 2½ miles

Getting there: The walk begins just off Moor Side Lane where there is a track signposted to Brontë Falls 1½ miles. On the opposite side of this road junction is Cemetery Road which goes to Haworth (1 mile). There is parking available here or just up the road at Stanbury Height (grid ref. 018361) where there are also picnic tables and toilets.

Go through the gateway and follow the Brontë Way track which takes you through the wonderful scenery of the South Pennine moors.

> To your right is Lower Laithe Reservoir and, on the left, Haworth Moor.

This track takes you all the way to Brontë Bridge. After a while the farm track becomes a narrower path and eventually begins to head downhill. There are some tricky sections of the path ahead; a small number of stone steps and an area of boulders. It is possible to push the pushchair down this section but we found it easiest to lift the buggy over the trickiest sections. After around 45 minutes you will

Brontë Bridge, Brontë Way

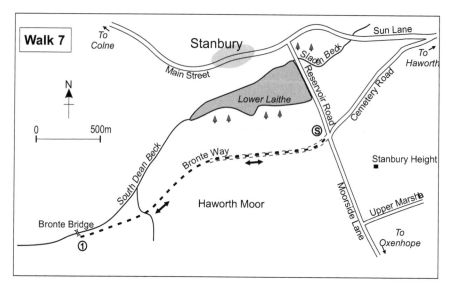

be able to see a stone footbridge over the stream (South Dean Beck). Before you get to the bridge there is a convenient flat grassy area on the left where you can leave the pushchairs.

1. The area around the bridge and stream is beautiful, especially on a hot summer's day, and well worth the effort to get to. Now is the time to get out your packed lunch and take the kids for a paddle in the stream.

To get back to your car, simply go back along the track you came in on.

In the area

If you are interested in literature, Haworth is the place to be. Visit the **Brontë Parsonage Museum** and walk around the town to see the sites connected with the Brontë sisters.

Take a trip on a steam trains on the **Keighley and Worth Valley Railway** (www.kwvr.co.uk or telephone 01535 645 214), which is open every weekend throughout the year and every day in summer. This railway was built in 1867 and was used in the filming of E. Nesbit's *The Railway Children* in 1970.

Walk 8: St Ives, Bingley

Allow: 1 hour 30 minutes

This is a good all-round walk, with lots to do and see along the way. The terrain is varied and some of the views are superb. Coppice pond is great for feeding the ducks, there's a lovely children's play area and a new café with a sunny terrace. The St Ives Estate used to be owned by the Ferrand Family, who lived there from the early 17th century. As you walk round, you will see an obelisk dedicated to William Ferrand; and nearby is Lady Blantyre's Rock, where William's mother in law used to sit and read.

Map: Ordnance Survey 1:25000 Explorer 288 – grid reference 095389

Distance: 3 miles

Getting there: Turn in to the main entrance of St Ives Estate off the B6429, and follow the road up until you see the park on the right and some wooden sculptures on the left. Park here.

Facing the wooden sculptures, turn right, following signs for Bingley St Ives Golf Club. After a couple of minutes, you will pass the golf club on your right and see some white chain links. Turn right past the white chains, following the signs for Golf Club and Public Car Park.

Soon the road bends to the right and the terrain starts to get a bit rougher here. Watch out for flying golf balls as the trail leads straight through the fairway! After about five minutes, the road forks to the left with a 'Private – golfers only' sign. Keep straight ahead, passing through an open gate.

1. Soon you will pass a small path to the right called Blind Lane. Ignore this and keep going straight, towards a green barn door.

   If it's a clear day, you should see a view of Bingley and the Damart chimney from here.

After about ten minutes you will see a kissing gate on the left.

Wood carving of Lady Blantyre

Before you go through this gate, look over the wall on your right and you should just about be able to spot a carving of a druid.

Go through the kissing gate, where the path gets a little rougher, but is lined with lovely rhododendrons (May/June). Eventually this path moves into woodland.

2. About fifteen minutes after the kissing gate, the footpath bends to the left. Keep to the fenced path, ignoring the smaller paths, which just lead to the fairways. There are a few benches dotted along this next stretch of downward path.

Eventually you will see some heath land on your right. At the end of this heath land, there is a small, faint path going off to the right. Ignore this and keep to the main trail. It soon starts to become quite a steep downhill slope.

A few minutes from there, you will see Lady Blantyre's Rock on your right (read stone slab for details). There are also some steps, which, if feeling energetic are worth a climb as there is a nice

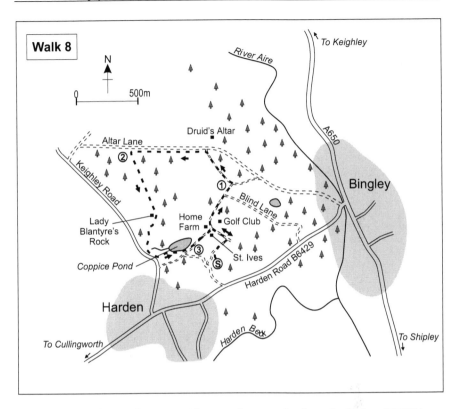

picnic table at the top. Also at the top is the obelisk of William Ferrand (again, details etched on stone).

Carry on down the path, which bends naturally to the left as you reach the flatter ground. After about ten minutes you will come to Coppice Pond. There are plenty of places to stop and feed the ducks here.

3. The path finally comes to a wooden gate, with a side exit at the left. Go through this and turn left to re-join the tarmac road, taking note of two-way traffic. In a couple of minutes you will see a café on your left. A great place for pram-pushers to re-charge!

Continue along this road and you will shortly come to the Golf Club again, where you will see the spot where the walk began. Keep going and eventually you will reach the car park, where there's a great kids play area, some more picnic tables and your car.

In the area

Bingley is a small town, which is slowly being redeveloped as the 'Bingley Bypass' has taken away a lot of the heavy traffic. Bingley **Five-Rise Locks** is good for a canal walk with a café along the way. If you fancy really getting into the Ferrand tradition, there's the **Ferrands Arms** pub, just near Bingley Arts Centre!

Walk 9: Shipley Glen, Baildon

Allow: 1 hour 30 minutes

This is a lovely walk through a picturesque wooded valley which has been a popular beauty spot since late victorian times. In its heyday Shipley glen was a large leisure park, featuring the aerial runway, a camera obscura and switchback railway to name but a few attractions. Thousands of people visited each day especially after the construction of the Shipley glen tramway in 1895. Little now remains to remind us of the previous popularity of this area. However, it is still possible to take the tramway down the hill to Saltaire.

This is a perfect spring walk as you pass through beautiful woodland carpeted with bluebells. Look out for ornate features within the wood dating back to the Victorian era and take in the fantastic views over Baildon moor. There are many tracks through the woodland making this walk worth revisiting time and time again. We have graded this as suitable for trainers, however the woodland paths can be uneven at times and muddy in wet weather.

Map: Ordnance Survey 1:25000 Explorer 288 – grid reference 132389

Distance: 2½ miles

Getting there: This walk begins at the Old Glen House pub on Glen Road, Baildon. Parking is available at several places along this road.

Walk down the hill from your parking spot to the pub. Turn right just before the public toilets (do not go down Prod lane). When you reach the pub turn right onto a small path into the woodland, do not follow the bridleway straight ahead.

There is a tea shop (Glen house tea rooms) and toilets next to the pub. At the end of Prod lane is Shipley Glen railway, a tramway that goes down the hill to Saltaire, a world heritage site (see walk 10).

Follow the path all the
way down into the
woodland until you
arrive at a junction in
a slight clearing with
a stile into a field on
your left.

The woodland floor is
covered in bluebells in
the spring.

Take the path that
goes ahead and then
bears to the left. Do
not turn sharp left or
go over the stile.

1. After a few minutes
   you come to a large
   pond surrounded by
   iron railings. Follow
   the path with the
   pond on your right

Shipley Glen

   and as you walk along
   you will see loadpit beck flowing out of the pond under the path.
   Once past the pond follow the small path around the fallen tree
   and then continue up the main track next to the dry stone wall.
   This track goes uphill through woodland for 10 mins and is the
   only strenuous part of the route. Half way up the path you will see
   an ornate iron gateway on your left, continue up the path, don't
   go through this gateway.

2. You will reach a bollard with a gold ball on top in the centre of the
   path. Ignore the footpath to your immediate right. Ahead of you is
   a fork in the track, take the right hand fork (Sheriff Lane) not the
   track to Gilstead.

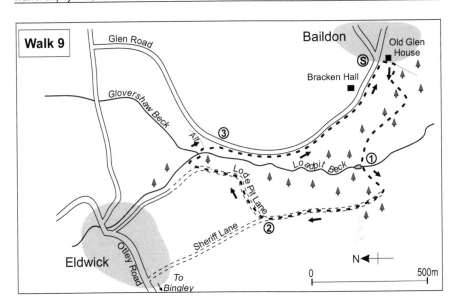

As you pass Broadstones Caravan park you will be able to see the village of Gilstead on the left and Baildon moor on the right.

Ignore all footpaths to the left and right and continue along the lane for 15 mins until you pass a farm on your right. Take the next right down Load pit lane and follow the path to the left past Glen lodge. The track then changes from gravel to tarmac. Follow this along ignoring paths to the right.

Turn right at the t-junction heading back into the woodland. Loadpit beck is on your left and ahead of you is a bridge. Go through the gateway at the end of the bridge and take the path to the right at the base of a large heather covered mound! This track is a bit rocky so watch your step.

If you have time for a diversion go left after the gateway and seek out the cup and ring marked stones (grid refs 131401 & 138403). The meaning of these carvings is disputed but they are thought to have been made 4 -5,000 years ago placing them in the Neolithic and bronze ages).

3. This path takes you back to Glen road. Head back down this road towards your car. You can follow the road or one of the many tracks on the grassy top of the glen. Be careful near the edge of the glen as the sides are very steep. It should take 10-15 mins to get back to your car and then it just remains to buy an ice cream from the conveniently parked van and the walk is complete!

Just before you reach the end of the walk you will come to Bracken Hall countryside centre on the left of Glen road. Entry is free and there is a small wildlife garden outside and information on local history, wildlife and other walks in the area within. There are also the remnants of an iron age stone circle outside the visitor centre.

In the area

Shipley Glen cable tramway (http://www.glentramway.co.uk) was built in 1895 and is the oldest working tramway in the UK. Two canopy topped trams travel up and down the steep wooded hill between Shipley glen and Saltaire. It is open most weekend and bank holiday afternoons and has a Santa special in december when the woodland is decorated with cartoon characters. At the bottom of the tramway is a small museum, a park, the river Aire and a waterbus on the canal as well as the delights of Saltaire.

Walk 10: Salt's Mill - Leeds Liverpool Canal via Hirst Wood, Saltaire

Allow: *45 minutes or 1 hour 30 minutes*

This walk is a perfect mixture of flat terrain, wooded paths and an historic residential area. It finishes back at Salts Mill, where you can treat yourself to either a full meal or just an ice cream. The beauty of these two walks is that you don't have to decide whether you want the longer or the shorter one until you are half way around!

In December 2001, Saltaire was designated a World Heritage Site by UNESCO. It is a purpose-built "model" Victorian industrial village built in the 19th century by the Victorian philanthropist Sir Titus Salt. The idea behind the design was to provide self-contained living space for the workers at his woollen mills.

Today, Salts Mill is still a hive of activity, after being converted by the late Jonathan Silver into the "1853 Gallery". Inside there is a collection of works from the famous artist, David Hockney (born in Bradford), as well as a superb café and a variety of good specialist shops (homewares, outdoor pursuits, books etc). Incidentally, all the street names in Saltaire are named after members of Sir Titus Salt's family.

Map: Ordnance Survey 1:25000 Explorer 288 – grid reference 143379

Distance: 1½ or 2¾ miles

Getting there: Park in the Visitors' Car Park of Salts Mill.

Follow the signs to Salt's Mill. Pass through the car park and head towards the black wrought iron gates. You are at Salts Mill and the start of the walk.

1. Note the 'NO HGV' sign, and with that to your right, there will be Saltaire United Reformed Church across the road. Cross the road and head downhill (right) towards the 'New Mill NHS' sign. Turn

left at the bottom of this road, where you will see the canal path (also on your left).

Join this canal path, with the bus stop sign on your right and start walking away from Salt's Mill. Next to the bus stop is a tourist sign of Saltaire which gives you some background history to the town as well as a handy map to show where you are!

Along this canal path you will pass a sports club on your right and some allotments on the left. Roughly ten minutes along the canal path, you will come to some locks

Salt's Mill

and a horse barrier. Go through the barrier and carry on up the path. On the right there is Saltaire Garden Centre and Nursery.

2. It is here where you can decide how energetic you are feeling:

If you're ready for a nosey around a few shops and a bite to eat, go straight to the paragraph marked *** If you feel like extending the walk by half an hour through some lovely woodland, go to the paragraph marked +++

+++ Cross the bridge on your left and turn right in to the car park. There are some picnic tables here. Head towards a kissing gate, which is the entrance to Hirst Wood. Go through the gate

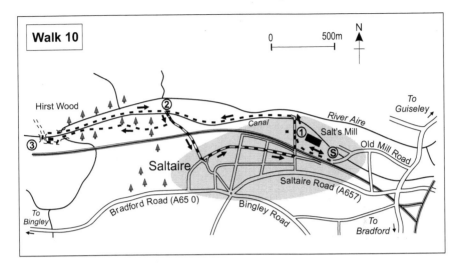

and keep to the right-hand path, heading upwards. There are many paths and trails through Hirst Wood, this is just one route, which takes about half an hour.

In a short while, the path forks. Follow the right-hand path. After a few more minutes, take the faint fork to the right-hand side. You need to keep your eyes open here as you could miss it. Look out for a couple of boulders further along on the right, about 10 yards up and check the large holly bush is on your left. This track starts getting pretty muddy with tree roots making it a bit tricky to manoeuvre.

Eventually, you will see a bench on your left and it will look like the path comes to an end. It doesn't. The next bit is quite tricky. The path gets much steeper and is very rocky. Go down this path and rejoin the canal path at the bottom, still heading away from Salts Mill.

3. Shortly, you will come to a house, where the path dips to the left. Follow this path around (with the sewage works on your left) until you come to another bridge. Cross over the bridge and turn right, rejoining the canal path, heading back towards Salts Mill. From here the terrain is easy going.

There are often ducks around here to stop and feed if you want a breather. The River Aire passes underneath the Leeds Liverpool canal here.

After about five to ten minutes along this path, you will come back to Saltaire Garden Centre and Nursery.

*** Cross the bridge over the canal on your left, opposite Saltaire Garden Centre and Nursery. And follow the pavement upwards.

Soon you will see a children's play area on your left, which is ideal if you've got a toddler. Take a left after this playground onto Dallam Avenue and continue straight on.

Keep going across the road, which turns into Caroline Street. Finally you will come to the main street called Victoria Road with a variety of shops and cafés. On your left should be Rance, Booth & Smith Architects. Turn left here and pass over the railway bridge. To your right is Salts Mill where the walk began.

In the area

Salt's Mill has a great café which is very child-friendly with plenty of high chairs, changing facilities and friendly staff who are happy to heat up any baby food you bring! And if your little darlings are behaving themselves, why not take a gander round the whole mill?

Just off the main roundabout in Saltaire is **'Jimmy G's'**, a children's soft play area, telephone 01274 533 848 for more details.

Shipley swimming baths is not far off and has a good-sized children's pool. Telephone 01274 437 162 for opening times.

Walk 11: Chellow Dean Reservoir, Bradford

Allow: 1 hour

Chellow Dean Reservoir is a good, easy walk with just one very small (but steep) hill. There are lots of ducks to feed and the walk incorporates some lovely stretches of woodland. This walk also includes a slight extension of about fifteen minutes.

This urban oasis is maintained by Bradford Council purely for leisure and wildlife. The reservoir is situated within the border of Bradford and shows that you don't have to go far out of town in order to find a quiet spot and get a breath of fresh air. The reservoir is a haven for wildfowl and is surrounded by woodland which shelters it from the surrounding urban expanse.

Map: Ordnance Survey 1:25000 Explorer 288 – grid reference 124345

Distance: 1½ miles

Getting there: Park on Chellow Lane, as high up as you can get.

Once you have got your pram and baby sorted, go through the red gate to the large house where you will see the reservoir. This circular walk can be done either way round.

Take the right-hand path, following the signs for circular walk with the reservoir on your left. Keep to this path all the way around, passing a set of steps on your right.

1. Shortly after passing these steps, there is a u-bend to your right with a steep, but short incline. Turn right and follow this path to the top. At the top, take the path straight ahead so that soon the reservoir will be on your right.

   This is a nice wooded area with lots of birds and ducks to look at.

2. If you want to add on an extra fifteen minutes or so, take the next

Lower Reservoir, Chellow Dean

left down a wooded path and keep going straight on until you see the main road ahead. Then turn around and come back to this same spot.

If you do not want to add on the extra length, turn right where you see the sign warning: blue green algae blooms and follow the path down with the stream on your right.

After about another fifteen minutes on this path, you will go up a small ramp and turn right, passing through both reservoirs (one on either side). Then take the left steep path down again and turn right at the bottom. Follow this path all the way to the end and turn left at the end of the reservoir by the railings. You will see the large house straight ahead where the walk began.

In the area

There are all kinds of child-friendly things to do in Bradford, most of which are aimed at children slightly older than pram-pushing age.

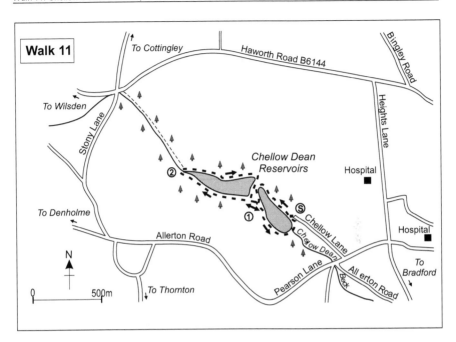

Possibly the most famous is **The National Museum of Film, Photography and Television** in the centre of Bradford, www.nmpft.org.uk. It has everything you could think of to do with film, photography and television including an Imax cinema and an area set up so that children can pretend to read the news on TV. For more information, call 01274 202 030.

Walk 12: Ogden Water, Bradford

Allow:: 45 minutes

There are many different woodland trails to take around Ogden Water, but we have gone for simplicity on this one, sticking to the main path all the way round. Obviously, you can choose whichever offshoots you like. It's a nice easy one with plenty to look at and picnic tables towards the end of the walk when you need re-fuelling. It is worth noting here that although there are toilets, they did not have baby-changing facilities at the time of writing.

Ogden Water is a 34 acre (14 hectare) reservoir, enclosed by 174 acres (70 hectares) of woodland. The Ogden estate was designated a local nature reserve in 2003. A quarter of a million people visit the area each year.

Map: Ordnance Survey 1:25000 Explorer OL21 – grid reference 066309

Distance: 1½ miles

Getting there: Park in the main car park, off Ogden Lane.

Ogden Water

Head down towards the reservoir, near the visitor centre.

1. Walk past the visitor centre on your right and go straight on through the gate, over the dam. At the other side of the dam, go through the gate on your right-hand side and follow the path round to the right. Basically, stick to this main path all the way round the reservoir.

2. After about twenty minutes or so, you will see a green bridge on your right. Cross over the bridge, turning right at the end and keep to the path with the reservoir on your right.

In another ten minutes or so, turn right again over another green panelled bridge, and follow the reservoir round. Very soon there is a fork in the road, with a sign left to the Woodland Trail. Keep to the main path here.

After roughly five minutes, there's a clearing with a picnic bench on your right, with lovely views over Ogden Water.

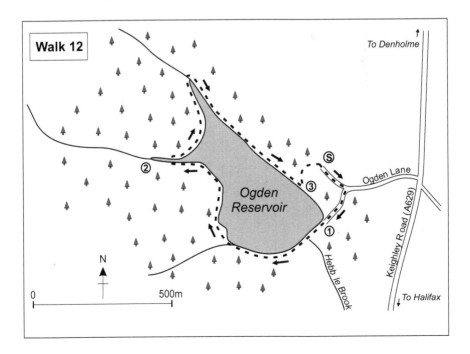

3. Continue following the path until you reach a wooden gate (with a bench on the left). Go through the gate and turn left up the path which winds round back to the car park.

Soon you will see two signs on your left, one to the reservoir, and another to the woodland trail. Just turn right as if doing a u-turn here. Look out for the carved wooden toadstools nearby. Then go through the wooden kissing gate at the top of the path and you are back in the car park.

In the area

In nearby Denholme is **Foster Park**, Foster Park View, Denholme, BD13 4LN. It's a children's playground with the added bonus of animals to see at the allotments just next to the park. For more information call 01274 437028.

Nearby is the **Manor Heath Park & Jungle Experience**, (visit www.calderdale.gov.uk/manorheath). This is actually in Halifax, just next to Saville Park, but it's worth a few extra miles to get there as it's free! There are tropical gardens with exotic flowers and butterflies, a walled garden and children's play equipment. For more information call 01422 365 631.

Walk 13: Leeds & Liverpool Canal, Apperley Bridge

Allow: *2 hours 30 minutes*

A nice, easy flat saunter along the Leeds & Liverpool canal with a pub stop half way – what more could you ask for? There are lots of barges to nosey at, some ducks to feed along the way and if you're lucky, a few cows or horses in the nearby fields to point out.

The neighbouring town of Calverley has long been associated with the wool industry. For centuries there was a manorial mill close to the packhorse bridge. The wooden swing bridge across the Leeds Liverpool canal, near the end of the walk is a grade two listed structure.

Map: Ordnance Survey 1:25000 Explorer 288 – grid reference 189379

Distance: 5 miles

Getting there: Park on Apperley Road, near the bridge over the canal.

Barges on the Leeds and Liverpool Canal

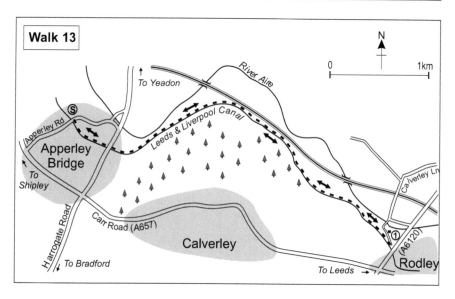

Facing the bridge, with the locks on your right-hand side in the distance, go left along the towpath, walking away from the locks. Soon you will go under a bridge. Keep straight on, following signs for Calverley Millennium Way.

After about an hour, you will come to a black gate and a horse barrier. Go through the horse barrier and follow the canal path straight on.

1. After few minutes, go through another barrier and eventually you will see the Railway Pub on your left, just away from the canal.

    At the Railway Pub there are baby-changing facilities, high chairs and an outdoor children's play area next to the beer garden. However, at the time of writing, they did not serve food on Mondays.

    Alternatively, you could keep walking along the canal path into Rodley, where there are other places to eat.

    There are also a few benches dotted along the side of the canal towards the end of this walk, so you could always have your picnic there.

When you have either had a pub lunch, a picnic or whatever,
simply turn back on the path and walk the same way back.

In the area

Cotton Budz soft play centre is in nearby Rodley at: 54(a) Oaklands
Road, Rodley, LS13 1LQ, telephone 0113 257 1188. This is a great
place for crawling babies and children up to about the age of seven to
let off some steam after sitting in a pram! There is a café with free
toast for the young ones before 10.30am and free juice all day. They
are also happy to heat up meals or bottles. Phone ahead for opening
times and prices.

Walk 14: Roundhay Park, Leeds

Allow: 1 hour 30 minutes

This is a perfect Sunday afternoon walk as it isn't too strenuous. There are lots of interesting things to see along the way (castle ruins, lakes, ducks to feed, children's playground) and to top it all off, about three-quarters of the way round, the Lakeside Café does great food, has baby changing facilities and even a bar! It is worth noting that this is just one route around the park - as you will see, there are many paths to take.

Set in 700 acres (283 hectares), Roundhay Park was bought by Leeds City Council in 1872 and opened by the third son of Queen Victoria, Prince Arthur. At the time, it was thought that it was a 'bad buy' as it was too far out of Leeds for the townsfolk to come and visit. Now of course, it is very popular.

Map: Ordnance Survey 1:25000 Explorer 297 – grid reference 327382

Distance: 2½ miles

Getting there: Park in one of the streets near The Roundhay Fox pub. There is a pay and display car park nearby, but we preferred the cheaper option!

The walk begins with The Roundhay Fox Pub on your left-hand side and Tropical World across the road. Follow the pavement downhill and turn immediately left in to the park over some cobbles, heading towards the bandstand. Take the left-hand path from the bandstand, heading upwards. After a few minutes, you will see Roundhay Mansion in front of you – go right at this T-junction, then take your next left, then left again, so you are walking past the mansion on your left.

At the next T-junction, go straight across following signs to 'Upper Lake'.

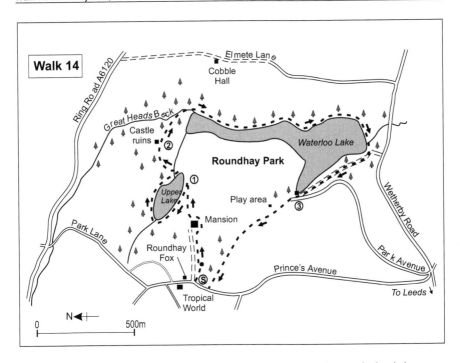

You will see another bandstand ahead to the right and the lake to left, where you can feed the ducks.

1. Keep following this path taking a sharp left as if going back on yourself. The lake should now be on your right. Follow this path along the edge of the lake all the way round.

There are lots of benches around both the upper and lower lakes for bottle-stops or quick breathers.

After about ten minutes there's a lovely wooden bridge. If you look over to the left, you can see a waterfall and a lower bridge, which you will cross shortly. Cross over this bridge and take your next left, following the sandy path, which snakes downwards. Keep straight on this path for about fifteen minutes, ignoring any smaller paths to either side.

2. Soon you should see the castle ruins. Go through the arch and join the main path again at the other side which heads right,

Castle ruins, Roundhay Park

taking you through a more wooded area (you can also see the lower lake to the right from here). In a short while, you will cross over a bridge with the stream running underneath. Turn right over the bridge and in a minute or two you will come to the lower lake. Take a left here, so the lower lake is on your right-hand side and just stick to the lakeside path, walking away from the castle ruins.

After about ten to fifteen minutes, you will see lots of boulders damming up the lake. Take a right, following the path over the dam. Once you have crossed over the dam, take a right, following the tarmac path towards the Lakeside Café.

The Lakeside Café not only has baby-changing facilities, but also sells alcohol! You will also see a playground straight ahead.

3. To continue the walk, go past the Lakeside Café and follow the left-hand side path upwards, with the playground to your right. Keep to the path until you get to the top and turn left towards the wrought iron gates and main road. When you go through the gate,

turn right, where you will shortly see the Roundhay Fox pub, where the walk began.

In the area

Tropical World – where you can follow the Amazon trail to see over thirty types of butterflies, owl monkeys, fruit bats, insects and reptiles. There is also a gift shop and café. If you go in spring/summer, you can see great flowerbed displays too, telephone 0113 266 1850.

The Canal Gardens - not actually a canal, but a long, rectangular pond, full of wildlife and with banks of flowers either side. There is no entry fee for The Canal Gardens.

Walk 15: Bramham Park, Bramham

Allow: 2 hours

Bramham Park is a magical place where you can explore 17th century gardens which remain virtually unchanged to this day. As you wander through the formal gardens the criss-crossing paths allow you to catch glimpses of the house and monuments. Take a picnic along as there are ample opportunities to stop and plenty of space for the kids to play. Go midweek and you may well have the gardens to yourself!

Lord Bingley, treasurer to both Queen Anne and King George II, created the estate to his own design after a tour around Europe. He was succeeded by his daughter Harriet Fox Lane who was responsible for the building of many of the monuments and obelisk. The estate has had a troubled past during which a fire gutted the house; however, the gardens have remained virtually untouched. The house has since been restored and Lord Bingley's descendants still live at Bramham and continue to maintain the estate to its original design.

Map: Ordnance Survey 1:25000 Explorer 289 – grid reference 409416

Distance: 3½ miles

Getting there: Drive in to the estate via the main entrance next to Bowcliffe Hall and park in the visitor's car park at the side of the house. There are toilets with baby changing facilities here.

Make your way to the information and refreshments point, which is signposted up the side of the house.

The grounds are open daily from 11.30am – 4.30pm from 1ˢᵗ April until 30ᵗʰ September. They are closed during the horse trials and the Leeds festival so check the website for details, www.bramhampark.co.uk. There is an entrance fee (£4 at the time of writing) but it is well worth it! Basic refreshments can be purchased here.

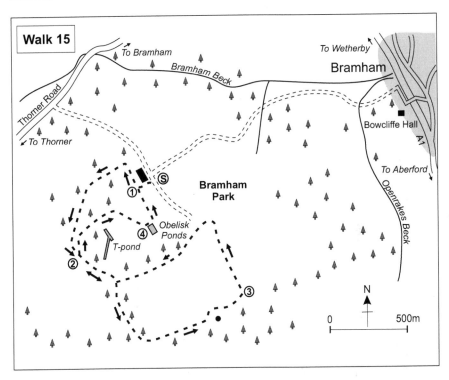

1. You will be directed through a room into the rear courtyard of the house. As you exit the house turn left onto the courtyard and then right onto a gravel path. This path takes you past the rear of the house with the Parterre on your left.

When you reach the small chapel ahead turn left up the grassy path with the tall beech hedge on your right. As you go up the beech lined avenue you will pass a statue, The Nymph, in a grassy quadrangle. Follow the path ahead and as you go round the corner you will pass a second statue, The Four Faces. Take the path straight ahead here.

After a few minutes you will see an area of woodland ahead. Follow the path into the woods; do not take path to the open temple on the left. The mown grass path takes you around the far edge of the woodland. Keep following the path around until you see a gateway on your right which will take you out of the formal garden area into a large grassy field.

2. Take the path diagonally left across the field down to a white gravel path. Turn right along the gravel path which takes you up through an avenue of trees. You will soon arrive at a junction where you must continue straight ahead up a small slope. At the next junction turn left along the public footpath, not straight ahead into Black Fen Wood.

The woodland ahead is marked as private but is open to anyone that paid to enter the estate. It is well worth a look if you have time and contains many paths to the temples and an obelisk.

The footpath takes you between a meadow and Black Fen Wood. Occasionally clearings in the wood will reveal some of the architecture within. Eventually you will come to a T-junction. Keep following the footpath to the left and not the white gated entrance to the woods.

3. As you go down the footpath you arrive at another junction. Go straight down the hill back into the private estate. Don't follow the footpath to the right. Follow the path down and round to the left. Take the next left into the woods, not the right-hand path which only takes you back to the visitor's car park.

You will soon see the Cascades below the Obelisk Ponds on your right. In the distance on your left are the Round Temple and the Obelisk.

After another five minutes you will arrive at the point where you first stepped on to the white gravel path. At this point take the grassy path back up towards the formal gardens – don't turn left back up the tree-lined avenue.

Once you have crossed the field go back through the gateway on your right into the garden area. Then follow the path straight ahead into the wood. This takes you through to a clearing and the Open Temple. Follow the beech-lined avenue down into the gardens. As you walk down you will see the T-shaped pond on your right and views over to Black Fen Wood.

Keep following the path straight ahead. There are many

Gothic Temple, Bramham Park

criss-crossing paths through the gardens along which you will see glimpses of monuments and the house. Once you see the house on your left bear right down a beech hedge-lined path.

4. The path brings you to a junction with another Gothic Temple on your right. Head left here down to the Obelisk Ponds and turn left onto the gravel path. Follow the path and then turn left heading past the herbaceous border and back to the house and the court-yard where we started the walk.

In the area

Lotherton Hall is situated to the south-east of Bramham and is an Edwardian gentleman's country residence with formal gardens and parkland. There is a bird garden with over 200 species of birds and red deer and rare breed cattle grazing in the parkland. The gardens and park are open daily dawn to dusk. For details of house and bird garden opening times see www.leeds.gov.uk/lothertonhall or telephone 0113 264 5535.

Walk 16: Lotherton Hall – Coburnhill Wood, Aberford

Allow: *1 hour 15 minutes*

This is a great short walk through beautiful woodland. There is plenty to see on this nature trail so pick up a leaflet from the estate shop and see what wildlife you can spot on the way round.

Lotherton Hall was the Edwardian country home of the Gascoigne family. Records suggest that there has been a hall on this site since at least 1086. The Gascoigne family purchased the hall in 1825 but it did not take on its present form until Colonel Frederick Gascoigne inherited the estate in 1893. The estate was given to Leeds Council in 1968 and has since been run as a museum with frequent exhibitions on fashion and local artists.

Map: Ordnance Survey 1:25000 Explorer 289 – grid reference 450361

Distance: 2½ miles

Getting there: Leave your car in the car park of Lotherton Hall Estate.

Walk up between the stables courtyard and Lotherton Hall following the signs for the formal gardens and estate walk.

1. When you see Lotherton Hall on your left, continue straight ahead along a paved path signed to the estate walks. Do not turn left towards the hall and formal gardens. After a few minutes go through the gate at the end of the paved path and go straight ahead ignoring gateways to the left and right.

   Go through the anti-horse barrier at the bottom right-hand corner of the field. Do not take the path at the bottom left corner of the field which takes you onto the estate boundary walk. Follow the path straight ahead down the edge of a field until you come to a gateway into the woodland. Do not take the path to the left part-way down the field.

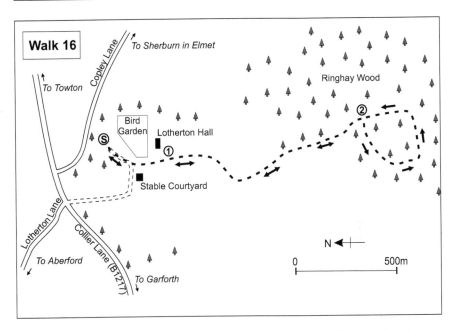

2. Go through the gate and follow the woodland path straight ahead. Pass through a second gate and after a few minutes you will come to a junction. Turn right along the path signposted as Coburnhill Wood walk 1 mile circular route (red marker).

After just a few minutes you will come to a slight clearing. Take the small path on the left back into the woodland, not the path ahead. As you follow the path round you will arrive at a cross-roads. Turn left here before the bench on the red marked trail.

Follow this narrow dirt path until you come to a T-junction and turn left along the red marked path. This path brings you back to the junction at the start of the circular wood walk. Go straight ahead here, through two gateways and out of the wood.

Follow the path on the right-hand side of the field back up to the estate, do not take any turnings to the right. This brings you back to the anti-horse barrier where you go straight across the field and through the gateway ahead. Follow the paved path back up to the Hall.

Lotherton Hall

In the area

There is plenty to do at **Lotherton Hall Estate** (www.leeds.gov.uk/lothertonhall or telephone 0113 264 5535). The Hall itself has been made into a museum exhibiting paintings, furniture and much more. Further walks can be done around the estate boundary and deer park as well as the formal gardens. There is a restaurant and an ice-cream kiosk in the stables courtyard as well as toilets with baby changing facilities.

Lotherton Hall Bird Gardens are well worth a visit. They have over 200 species of rare and endangered birds. It is home to the world's largest land-based bird, the Andean Condor!

Walk 17: Temple Newsam, Leeds

Allow: 2 hours

Temple Newsam is a fantastic Tudor-Jacobean mansion set within a large estate. The estate contains a mixture of parkland, woodland and formal gardens landscaped by Capability Brown in the 18th century. This was the birthplace of Lord Darnley, husband of Mary Queen of Scots, and then family home to the Ingrams for over 300 years. The estate is now managed by Leeds City Council and entry to the grounds is free for all.

This is a great walk taking in a mixture of all three landscape types within the park. You get to see the house and formal gardens before heading out towards the woodland and the estate perimeter. There is plenty of space for the kids to run around and ample opportunities for picnics. Check out the Temple Newsam website www.leeds.gov.uk/templenewsam or telephonoe 0113 264 5535 for details of opening times and facilities.

Map: Ordnance Survey 1:25000 Explorer 289 – grid reference 360324

Distance: 4 miles

Getting there: Park in Home Farm car park within the Temple Newsam Country Park which is just off Junction 46 of the M1.

Walk along the cobbled path between the animal enclosures with the farm buildings on your right. At the gateway at the end of this path turn right and follow the road up to the front of Temple Newsam House.

You will pass the Stables Courtyard and Home Farm on your right where there is a reception, shop, tea rooms and toilets with basic baby changing facilities. As you continue to walk up to the house you will be able to see Avenue Wood and a small temple in the distance on your left.

Temple Newsam

1. Once you have passed the house you will come to a T-junction, turn left along a narrow avenue with the house behind you. Continue along this track passing a sign for Pegasus wood and Avenue.

There are numerous paths into the formal garden area from this avenue. There are benches on the top of the grassy bank that you will pass on your left from where there are great views over Leeds.

When you come to a crossroads keep on the dirt path straight ahead, not the gravel or tarmac paths to the left and right. Follow this path along between two hedges until you come to a gateway where you turn left on to a dirt track.

After about five minutes you will come to a crossroads, take the route straight ahead along the Bullerthorpe Lane Temple Newsam bridleway. As the track bends to the left turn right through the horse barrier which takes you on to the path towards The Avenue and Bullerthorpe Lane.

2. Go up the grassy path following it along the edge of the woodland

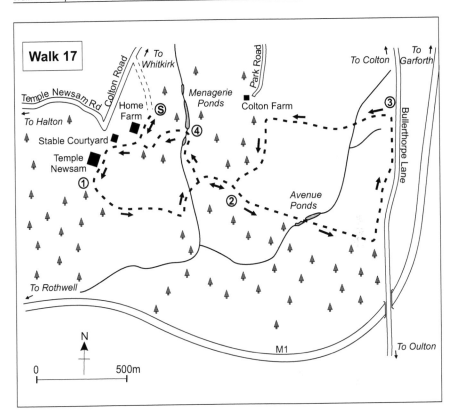

on the left. This brings you to a gravel path which takes you up a long avenue with great views of Temple Newsam House behind you. Pass over the Avenue Ponds and continue almost to the end of the path. When you see the road ahead of you turn left through a horse barrier and gate. At the next junction follow the Temple Newsam bridlepath straight ahead.

3. After ten minutes you will come to a junction and turn left down the Temple Newsam and Colton Bridleway. This brings you almost immediately to a fork in the path where you turn left again. The gravel path then takes you past a barrier gate and back down towards Temple Newsam House.

Go through the next gateway and follow the public footpath to Colton straight ahead. At the T-junction take the Temple

Newsam bridlepath to the left. This brings you back to a section of the track you used just before you got to the Avenue. Follow the track as it bends to the right and then turn right at the next junction towards Lakes House.

4. Cross over the bridge and turn right off the main path, passing Menagerie Ponds on your right.

There are plenty of grassy secluded spots here where you could stop for a picnic.

Follow this path along ignoring turnings to the right. This brings you back to Home Farm, where you turn right along the cobbled path between the animal enclosures to the car park where, if you are lucky, you will find an ice-cream van!

In the area

Home Farm, www.leeds.gov.uk/templenewsam or telephone 0113 264 5535, is working rare breeds farm that is open to the public. Take your kids to meet the animals, help out at feeding time and take part in craft demonstrations.

Middleton Railway, www.middletonrailway.org.uk or telephone 0113 271 0320, founded in 1758, is the world's oldest railway and trains run every weekend from April to December. The railway runs to another of Leeds parks, Middleton Park, where there is a nature trail, lakes and picnic area.

Walk 18: Judy Woods, Wyke

Allow: 1 hour 45 minutes

This walk passes through some lovely woods and farmland but can be hard going at times with some rocky tracks. There are no café facilities or toilets along the way, so go prepared with snacks and drinks. It would also be better to tackle this one when the weather is dry as some of the paths could get quite muddy.

Judy Woods is the third largest woodland area in the Bradford district, boasting forty hectares of land. The name originates from Judy North or 'Gurt' Judy, who lived in a nearby cottage in the 1850s and 1860s. Judy was married to a chap called Joseph North, whose family tended the woods. When Joseph died, Judy took over as a gardener. It is also believed she used to sell sticks of spice and ginger beer to the passing walkers. Some of the beech trees in the woods are as old as two hundred years.

Map: Ordnance Survey 1:25000 Explorer 288 – grid reference 146267

Distance: 3 miles

Getting there: Park on Station Road, just off the A641, near the entrance of Judy Woods (by the kissing gate).

Go through the kissing gate and follow the main path straight ahead, ignoring any other small off shoots. After about fifteen minutes the path forks and there is a big tree stump in the middle. Take the right-hand fork and head towards the steel gate.

1. Turn right through the steel gate and follow the track upwards. Shortly you will go through two black metal posts, following the path ahead (don't be tempted to turn left into the woods). After about five minutes, you will pass a smallholding on your right called Woodside Farm.

2. Eventually the road widens out into a street. Turn left onto Carr

Low Wood, Judy Woods

House Gate (the sign for this is not immediately obvious as it is posted on the other side of the street!), opposite High Fernley Primary School. This road turns into a gravel track. You will pass houses on your right and a farm on the left further up.

Go right to the top of this track, where you will see a scrap yard. Keep going straight on along a small footpath. This path occasionally looks blocked as people dump some garden waste here. Once you are over that, the path narrows and gets a bit rocky. You will soon see a substation on your right. Keep straight on until you get to a T-junction at the end.

3. Turn left at the T-junction onto the tarmac lane. After about ten minutes, you will come to a steel gate on the left, which can be quite hidden with weeds. Go left here and follow the right-hand path downwards. The track is quite rocky here. At the end of this track, turn left and after about thirty seconds turn right through the steel gate, which you came through near the beginning of the walk (marker 1 on map). Follow this path straight back towards the kissing gate at the start of the walk.

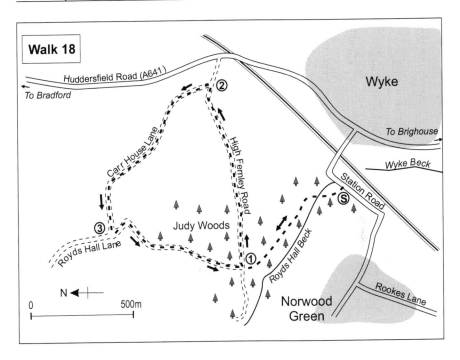

In the area

Why not take a trip to **Bradford City Farm** in nearby Girlington? Opening times can vary, so it is a good idea to ring ahead on 01274 543 500.

Or, if it's a hot day and you feel like taking the kids for a swim, try the **Richard Dunn Sports Centre**, Rooley Avenue, Bradford BD6 1EZ. Telephone 01274 307430.

Walk 19: Gibson Mill - Hardcastle Crags, Hebden Bridge

Allow: 1 hour 30 minutes

Take a leisurely saunter through this National Trust park and enjoy the woodland and all its wildlife. Look out for the harmless hairy wood ants which live in huge anthills beneath the conifer trees and can be seen crossing the many paths!

At the same time you have the opportunity to take a look back at our industrial past at Gibson Mill. This mill was built around 1800 and harnessed the power of Hebden Water to produce cotton cloth. The mill is now being restored by the National Trust and should be open to visitors in 2006. There will be a café and interactive exhibitions exploring the crags, the history of the mill and the green technology which the mill now uses to function.

Map: Ordnance Survey 1:25000 Outdoor Leisure 21 – grid reference 969298

Distance: 3 miles

Getting there: Park in the Clough Hole car park on Widdop Road between the villages of Slack and Ridge Nook.

Go out of the car park onto Widdop Road and turn left. In a few metres turn left again, just before the stream, through a gateway signposted as a public footpath to Hardcastle Crags.

Follow the track down the hill, going through two gateways and into the woodland. The track can be rocky in places so watch your step. Stay on this track to the bottom of the hill, which should take around 10 mins, ignoring the path you pass on your left. At the T-junction at the bottom of the hill turn left.

This area is filled with bluebells in the spring and on your right you will soon see Gibson Mill and Hebden Water.

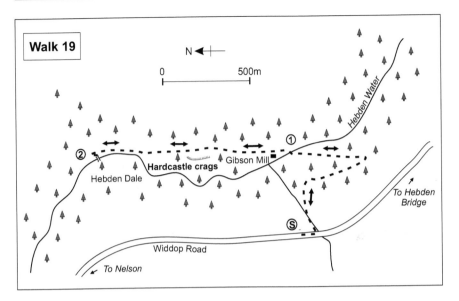

1. When you reach Gibson Mill cross the bridge over the river. Turn left onto the footpath passing the mill on your left.

   There are picnic tables down by the river next to the mill and benches along this path. As you go along this track you will see some large boulders to your left which form the top of the rocky outcrop of Hardcastle Crags.

   When you come to a fork in the track take the path to the left marked as a non-cycle route and go through the gate ahead of you.

2. After a few minutes take a small path to the left and you will come to a wooden bridge. The walk should have taken about 45 mins so far and this is the turning point.

   If it is a warm day this is a lovely place to find a spot next to the river for a picnic. If you are feeling adventurous it is possible to explore some of the track on the other side of the river from where you may be able to get a better view of the crag and of the fisherman's cave. However, some sections of the track are not suitable for pushchairs and, therefore, we must return to the car along the route we came in.

Footbridge over Hebden Water

Turn round and go back up the small track and turn right onto the main path at the top. Follow the track back to the mill and cross over the river. Turn left after the bridge and follow the path as it bears right uphill into the wood. Follow the path up the hill, through the gates and back to the car park.

In the area

Hebden Bridge is said to be one of the most 'cosmopolitan' centres of the north and has plenty of shops and cafés to keep you occupied for an afternoon.

Visit www.eureka.org.uk or telephone 01422 330069, for information on '**Eureka**' – a museum for kids which teaches them about themselves and the world around them, is situated in nearby Halifax. This fantastic museum has lots of interactive games and activities and is open 7 days a week, 10.00am – 5.00pm.

Walk 20: Mytholm – Colden Clough, Heptonstall

Allow: 2 hours

Heptonstall was once an important centre for the textile trade. The relics of this time can be seen in the Old Cloth Hall and the many pack-horse trails in the area. However, when mechanisation arrived the trade moved out of this town to Hebden Bridge with mills all along the rivers. There were 13 mills along Colden Water and you may be able to spot some of these as you walk along. Also, look out for Lumb Bank, where the late poet laureate Ted Hughes (1930-1998) once lived.

This is a great walk incorporating green lanes and woodland tracks. The start of the walk involves a steep climb but after that it is easy walking. The track back along Colden Clough can be quite rocky in places. There are great views over the surrounding valleys throughout the walk.

Map: Ordnance Survey 1:25000 Explorer OL21 – grid reference 983274

Distance: 3½ miles

Getting there: Park on Church Lane (just off the A646 Hebden Bridge to Todmorden road) opposite Bank Terrace.

Walk up the road with the terrace of houses on your right. This is a quiet country road but be careful as you may see the occasional car. The road winds its way up the hill. Do not go down the footpath to the left, next to Glen View, and ignore other small footpaths to the left and right.

1. After 5-10 minutes you will see a white gravel track on the left which veers sharply to the left. Walk up this bridleway and look out for the fantastic views of Calderdale through the trees. This track begins with a steep climb but levels out after 10 mins.

Winter's Lane bridleway

Once you come out of the trees you will be able to see Stoodley Pike monument on Higher Moor on the left.

Take the track on your right immediately after the first house you pass (Green Barn). At the end of the track go through the small gateway leading onto a grassy path between two stone walls. At the end of this path is another gate which takes you onto a lane. Follow this, ignoring all footpaths and lanes to the left and right.

2. Eventually you will come to a signposted junction in the path. Take the bridleway to the right towards Jack Bridge. After 10 minutes you will come to a road (Badger Lane). Turn left and then immediately right, just past the first house, up the Pennine bridleway towards Jack Bridge. This track is narrower than the previous one but also has great views.

3. After a steep downhill stretch, you will arrive at a house, take the tarmac lane to the left which brings you straight to a second junction. To continue the walk go right here with Colden Water on your left.

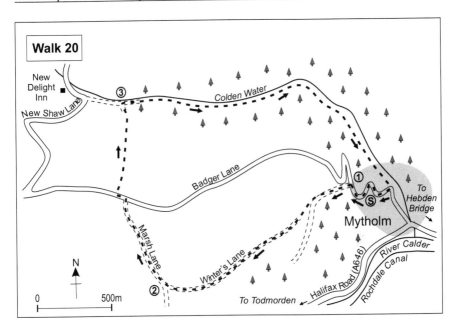

If you fancy a drink and a bite to eat at a pub go left here and after a 5-minute walk you will come to Smithy Lane, Jack Bridge. Cross the road to a children's play area and camp site ahead. Turn right and you will see the New Delight Inn which has a beer garden and serves food 12-2pm everyday except Monday. To return to the walk simply return along the same bridleway (signposted to Callis Bridge).

Take the stony track straight ahead; don't follow the tarmac lane to the house. Stay on this track ignoring all footpaths to the left and right. The track can be very stony in places so take care.

You will be able to see views of Heptonstall church ahead and Foster and Bob Woods on the other side of the river.

Veer right as the track joins a wider lane.

You will see a children's playground and picnic tables in a small park to the left. This can be reached by taking one of the narrow tracks

down through the trees or by continuing along on to Church Lane
and taking the road to the left immediately before the church.

At the end of the bridleway turn right onto Church Lane and walk
uphill for a short distance to your car.

In the area

If you have a bit of time to spare, why not walk the **history trail** and
visit the **museum** in Heptonstall? This takes you past the important
landmarks and tells of the history of the town's textile industry.

Alternatively take a horse-drawn trip up the **Rochdale Canal** and be
'legged' through one of the canal tunnels. Boats run all year from the
marina, Hebden Bridge – www.caldervalleycrusing.co.uk or telephone
01422 845 557.

Walk 21: Greetland Moor, Greetland

Allow: *1 hour 30 minutes*

Greetland is a small town to the south of Halifax in the heart of Calderdale. It is thought to have been the site of a Roman camp and a Roman altar (dated AD205) was found here. Greetland is also the start of the Calderdale Way, a 50-mile circular walk which takes you across moorland and packhorse trails around the Calder valley.

This is an easy walk along wide green lanes with great views over Calderdale. Apart from a few potholes the terrain is good throughout. There are a couple of pubs on route so why not bide your time and stop for refreshments!

Map: Ordnance Survey 1:25000 Explorer OL21 – grid reference 081213

Distance: 3 miles

Getting there: Leave your car on Moor Bottom Lane just off the B6113 Rochdale Road.

Walk up the gravel track away from the main road. Stay on this track ignoring footpaths to the left or right.

There are views of Greetland church to your right.

1. When you arrive at a cross roads take the left track. This is a dirt lane with many potholes. As you walk along you will pass Bilberry Hall and Greetland Moor on your left.

   Follow the track until you come to a road (Turbury Lane). Cross the road and turn right and in a few minutes turn down the bridleway on your left. This soon turns into a grassy track between a stone wall and a fence.

2. This track ends at Rochdale Road with a pub (The Sportsman's

Bridleway alongside the Sportsman's Inn, Rochdale Road

Inn) on the left. Cross the road and turn right, do not go down the footpath straight ahead. Walk along the pavement until you see Dog Lane on your left, signposted as a footpath to Wall Nook and Barsey Green. Follow this tarmac lane down past woods and houses, ignoring footpaths to the left and right.

When you reach a fork in the road, go left down the tarmac lane and not the gravel track ahead. This soon becomes a dirt and stone track. At the next fork take the left-hand track down to the road.

Turn left onto the road (Saddleworth Road) and walk along the pavement towards Greetland.

On the right are views across Stubbing Wood and the surrounding countryside.

3. You will soon come to the Branch Road Inn on your right and opposite this is a gravel track marked as a footpath. Turn left here and follow the track (Syke House Lane) past some houses. It soon

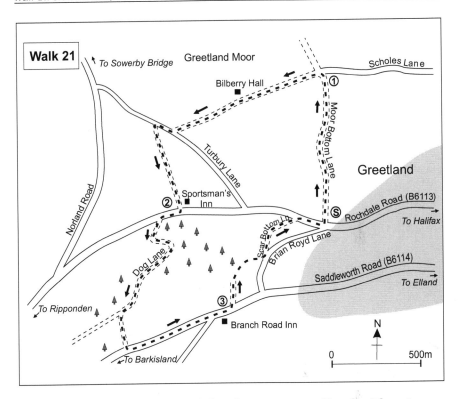

becomes a narrow dirt path heading into woodland with a stream on the left. Bear right at the T-junction, which brings you to a second junction where you go right again.

Follow this track to the road (Brian Royd Lane) and immediately turn left up Scar Bottom Lane. This is a gravel track with lots of potholes. Turn right at the T-junction and you will soon come back to Rochdale Road. Turn right here and walk along the pavement towards Greetland. After a few minutes cross the road and turn left up Moor Bottom Lane and find your car.

In the area

Manor Heath Park, Jungle Experience and Walled Garden, www.calderdale.gov.uk/manorheath or telephone 01422 365101, is just up the road in Halifax. Take a walk through the grounds, visit the various gardens and see the butterflies on display here.

Shibden Hall, www.calderdale.gov.uk/tourism/museums/shibden or telephone as above (01422 365101), is just off the A58 east of Halifax and is great for kids. Walk through the woodland or parkland, go on the children's rides or miniature railway and even take a boat out on the lake.

Walk 22: Slaithwaite to Marsden (Canal Walk)

Allow: *2 hours*

This is a perfect canal walk, which includes a pub at the end, followed by a nice quick train journey back. You do need two people though as there are some steep steps to get down onto the train platform. Alternatively, you could simply cut out the train journey and walk back the way you came.

Marsden is a Pennine mill town steeped in history. More recently it has been used for filming parts of 'Last of the Summer Wine' and 'Where The Heart Is'. It was also home to local poet Samuel Laycock. The canal was restored in 2001.

Map: Ordnance Survey 1:25000 Explorer 288 – grid reference 081141

Distance: 2¾ miles

Getting there: Park in the short stay car park just opposite Slaithwaite Co-Op, near the coffee shop and public toilets.

Get onto the pavement along Carr Lane, walking away from the car park, with the canal on your left-hand side. Go straight across the zebra crossing on Britannia Road (the one opposite Monsoon Tandoori Restaurant) and head down the canal path.

Within a minute, you come to the road again, go through the black metal bollards and keep straight on. You should see the first lock and a stone bridge on your right-hand side, with the River Colne on the left.

Look out for the 'Moonraker Floating Tearoom' coming up soon on your right. After about ten minutes, go through a metal kissing gate and continue straight on. You will get to another kissing gate about half an hour after this – do the same there.

Huddersfield Narrow Canal

1. Soon after the second kissing gate you will see Sparth reservoir to your left (just over the wall).

   You could venture down a small path for a nosey if you like, but we stuck to the main route. A few minutes after the reservoir you can see a pretty waterfall to your left.

2. Eventually, you will go under a bridge, just before you get to Marsden. Keep straight on until you go under a second bridge, where you will see The Railway Pub in front of you (with high chairs and baby changing facilities).

   It is worth checking train times back to Slaithwaite here, as when we did this walk they were only running hourly.

   After you have refreshed yourselves in the pub, come back to this spot and head upwards on the pavement with the train station to your right. Cross over the bridge at the top and go down the last set of steps to the platform for trains to Slaithwaite. This is where you definitely need two people.

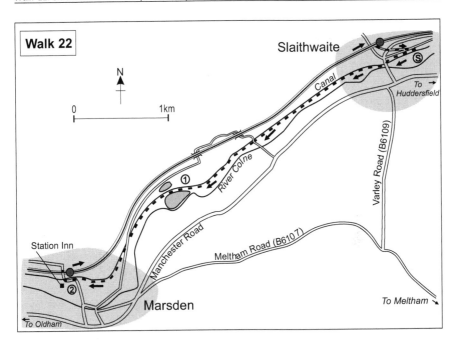

3. Get off the train at Slaithwaite, turn left and make your way down the hill, under the bridge. Cross over the road and turn right, continuing to follow the road downhill. Very soon, turn left onto Lewisham Road, where shortly you will see Slaithwaite Co-op on your left and the car park on your right.

In the area

Marsden Park has a great play area where the kids can get rid of some energy! There are also a handful of pleasant village shops.

Take a trip on a canal barge into **Standedge Tunnel**, the deepest, longest and tallest canal tunnel in the country. Trips leave from Marsden on weekends and bank holidays. For full details of opening times go to www.waterscape.com/servicesdirectory/Standedge_Tunnel or telephone 01484 845624.

If you fancy some more walking why not visit the National Trust's **Marsden Moor Estate**? Details are at www.nationaltrust.org.uk. This large moorland estate provides a wide variety of walking and the opportunity to spot some rare wildlife.

Walk 23: Last of the Summer Wine, Holmfirth

Allow: *1hour*

This is the sort of walk to tackle when you're feeling energetic as it begins with a very steep uphill climb. We would also say it's a 'fair weather' walk as some of the tracks downhill can get pretty muddy. However, the uphill climb is worth it for the great views over the Holme valley and you can treat yourself to a good lunch at the Wrinkled Stocking Café at the end of the walk.

The area of Holmfirth was made famous through the hit TV series *Last of the Summer Wine*. Although this walk takes you away from the centre of the village, if you pick up a leaflet from the Tourist Information Centre, you can spot all the main points of interest on your return - from Nora Batty's house to Sid's Café.

Map: Ordnance Survey 1:25000 Explorer 288 – grid reference 141082

Distance: 2½ miles

Getting there: Park in the centre of Holmfirth at the pay and display car park, which is next to the Tourist Information Centre.

Turn right out of the car park (away from the Tourist Information Centre) and keep going until you get to Ashley Jackson Galleries and Upperthong Lane. Turn right up Upperthong Lane.

This is a very steep hill and you will probably want a couple of breathers on the way.

1. Keep on going straight up until you get to what looks like a fork in the road. Take the left-hand turning on to Broad lane. After about another ten minutes up this hill (it *does* get easier, honestly!), turn right into Netherhouses, opposite a house called Sycamore Lodge.

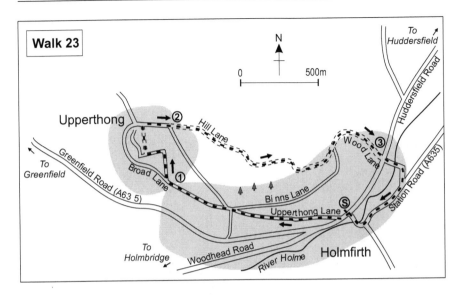

At the top of this short road, turn left at the T-junction onto Holme View Drive. When you get to house number 16 on your right, turn up the footpath just to the side of it. (This is the final push up. You can do it!) At the top of this footpath, turn right by the Royal Oak Pub – it's all downhill from now on.

2. After a few minutes, go left down Hill Lane on the public footpath.

   This takes you through all sorts of farm land and houses. There are also some lovely views over the Holme Valley.

   After about twenty minutes, the path becomes easier as you come across more houses. Keep going straight along Holt Lane through a no through road sign. Eventually you will see a huge pylon in front of you and a bench on the left. Turn right here, down the public footpath, which is quite narrow. Soon you will get to a gate with the sign Wood Farm. Go through the gate and keep heading downwards on Wood Lane, until you get to the main road (Huddersfield Road).

3. Cross over Huddersfield Road onto Bridge Lane. You will pass the Fire Station and Co-op on your right, and cross over the river.

Compo's Café

Follow the road round to the right-hand side, where there is another small uphill climb. When you come to the top of Bridge Lane, turn right at the junction, heading downwards again. In a few minutes you will come to the centre of Holmfirth.

You can stop for refreshments, a nosey around the shops or have a more in-depth look at the sites from the TV series *Last of the Summer Wine*. Disappointingly, at the time of writing this, the famous Sid's Café did not have high chairs and prams were not allowed inside. However, the staff are very helpful and will show you where to park your pram nearby.

To get back to the car park, keep straight on, passing the public toilets and the bus station. Turn right up Victoria Street. Then left at the T-junction onto Huddersfield Road. Soon you will see the Tourist Information Centre and car park again, where the walk began.

If you keep along this road for a few minutes, you will get to The Wrinkled Stocking Café, which has high chair facilities.

In the area

There are *Last of the Summer Wine* **TV tours** available, which take in all the sites in the area made famous through the hit TV series – from Sid's Café to Compo's home. There are also plenty of craft and antique shops and a good handful of children's clothing and toy shops.

Holmfirth holds a **Festival** once a year, with a special children's weekend. In 2005 it was held at the beginning of May. There are lots of things for children to do including Punch and Judy and Teddy Bears' Picnics. Check the website www.holmfirthfestival.com for more information or telephone 01422 833552.

Walk 24: Clayton West (Kirklees Light Railway) – Skelmanthorpe

Allow: 1 hour 30 minutes

If you fancy something fun and a little different then this is the walk for you. This trip incorporates a ride on a steam train with a walk through beautiful British countryside. This is definitely a fair weather walk as the dirt paths get very muddy in wet weather.

The Clayton West branch line was opened in 1879 to serve the coal industry as well as for passenger service. It went out of use in the 1970s when many of the mines were closing, but was reopened as a tourist attraction in 1991. So why not hop into a carriage and let Hawk, Owl, Badger or Fox steam their way through the enchanting countryside? Then take a leisurely stroll through local farmland back to Clayton West.

Map: Ordnance Survey 1:25000 Explorer 288 – grid reference 257112

Distance: 2¾ miles

Getting there: Find your way to the Kirklees Light Railway station at Clayton West (there are brown road signs directing you there).

Go to the visitor centre, where you can buy your tickets and board the train.

There is a café in the station that has high chairs and the staff are happy to heat up your baby food. There are also toilets with baby changing facilities and both indoor and outdoor children's play areas here. Trains run hourly at weekends throughout the year and daily between June and September – visit www.friendsofklr.co.uk or telephone 01484 865 727. You need to get off at Skelmanthorpe station (a 15-minute ride) so, if possible, let the driver know this before the train leaves.

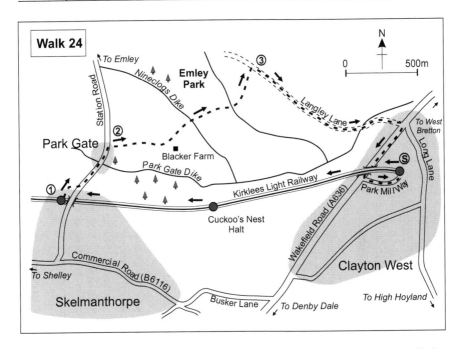

If you have time for a longer ride (40 minutes) the train goes all the way to Shelley and then will drop you off on the return trip. The guards are very friendly and will help you load the pushchairs into the carriage.

1. Leave the train at Skelmanthorpe station and take the path off the platform. Go straight over the road at the roundabout and head down the hill into the village. Continue through the village ignoring footpaths to the left. Cross the road and begin to head uphill.

2. As you pass the last house, take the track signposted as a public bridleway on the right. The track goes all the way to Blacker Farm, but just before you reach the farm gates, take the bridleway on the left. Go through the gate and then through a second gate straight ahead which leads into a field.

The bridleway follows the right-hand border of this field. Take the gate at the end of the field and follow the dirt track. Again, follow the path along the right-hand side of this field.

Kiirklees Light Railway, Skelmanthorpe Station

These paths follow dirt tracks and, therefore, would not be suitable for pushchairs in wet weather.

At the corner of the field go through the gateway and turn left. Go diagonally across this field passing through the gateway at the far corner. Follow the wall on the right and go through the gateway at the corner, which takes you onto a stony lane.

On the right you should be able to see Clayton West and on the left Emley Tower.

3. Turn right down the lane heading towards Clayton West. You will soon come to a T-junction in the path, turn left here and follow the lane down hill. At the end of the track you will see the Junction Inn. Turn right just before this following Langley Lane passing the pub on your left. Cross the main road carefully and turn right back towards the station. The railway is signposted on the left up Park Mill Way.

In the area

Cannon Hall museum, park and gardens, www.barnsley.gov.uk/tourism/cannonhall or telephone 01226 790270, are just a few miles down the road, across the county border in South Yorkshire. The hall is a museum exhibiting furniture, paintings, glassware and pottery. Have something to eat in the Victorian tearooms or take a picnic and walk through the extensive grounds.

Cannon Hall Open Farm – www.cannonhallfarm.co.uk or telephone 01226 790 427 – is adjacent to the museum. This award-winning farm has a large array of animals and birds and there are always plenty of baby animals to see. There is also an adventure playground, a gift shop and tea shop. In addition there is a farm shop on site so you can stock up your larder while you are there!

Walk 25: Stanley Ferry Canal, Wakefield

Allow:: *1 hour 30 minutes*

The terrain is easy on this canal and nature reserve walk. There are lots of interesting barge boats along the side of the canal (many are moored permanently). On top of that, this walk takes in Southern Washlands local Nature Reserve with wildlife a-plenty.

This is part of the Trans Pennine Trail. The construction of the Aire & Calder Navigation began in the 1700s to help with transport of wood and coal instead of using packhorses. From the 19th century, demand increased for a bridge. The original bridge at Stanley Ferry was constructed in 1879. The land along this canal and river represent one of the highest concentrations of designated nature areas in the Wakefield District. A lot of them were former industrial sites, which have been reclaimed.

Map: Ordnance Survey 1:25000 Explorer 289 – grid reference 354229

Distance: 2¾ miles

Getting There: Park in the Stanley Ferry Marina car park, near the Mill House pub.

Walk towards the Mill House pub and turn left down the small road at the side of the pub, which leads round to another car park at the bottom. Head to the bottom left-hand side of this car park, where you will see a small tarmac path leading upwards, which joins the canal.

1. At the top of this tarmac path, turn right, where you will see an information board with details of the surrounding conservation areas. On your left you should be able to see the famous Stanley Ferry Aqueduct in the distance.

   After about ten minutes, turn right through a white horse barrier by the sign, which says 'Stanley Ferry Visitor Moorings 85'. This

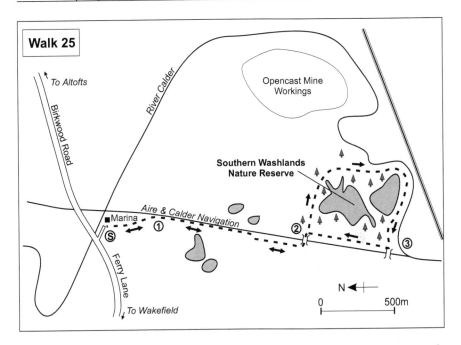

takes you away slightly from the canal. Eventually this path forks. Keep straight on (the left-hand fork), not upwards towards the fields.

2. In another five minutes or so, turn left over the bridge, crossing over the canal and head towards the green horse barrier on the right. Go through the barrier and turn left into the nature reserve. Basically, keep to the main path all the way around.

Soon you come to a small fork to the right. Keep straight ahead. After another few minutes, there's another fork – keep straight ahead here too.

You will be able to hear the River Calder weir from here and just up a little further on your left is a small clearing with a big log bench where you can see it cascading down. It's worth a look.

In another ten minutes, the path widens out with the River Calder on your left and a lake on your right. Soon this path stops as you are facing a big stone bridge.

Barges on the Aire and Calder Navigation

3. Turn right here before the bridge (along the main path, NOT directly alongside the canal).

Eventually, you will arrive back at the green horse barrier again. Go through the barrier and turn left, crossing back over the bridge and take the right-hand path back the way you came. Soon you will arrive at the white horse barrier, which means you are back to the canal. Turn left here (Stanley Ferry Visitor Moorings 85) and continue until you get to the pub car park again on your left, next to the information board. Turn left down the path and follow the car park road back to your car.

If you're peckish, the pub (The Mill House) is child-friendly with plenty of high chairs and baby-changing facilities.

In the area

A little bit further out is the **Waterton Discovery Centre and Anglers Country Park**, just near Wintersett reservoir. You can visit the bird hides, try to spot the heron or see if you can see any dragonflies. There is also a café and baby changing facilities too. For more information, call 01924 303 980.

Walk 26: Fairburn Ings Nature Reserve, Castleford

Allow: 2 hours 45 minutes

Fairburn Ings was designated a nature reserve in 1957 and is now one of the most important reserves in West Yorkshire, boasting the highest number of bird species for any inland UK site. Reclaimed from the spoil heaps of opencast mine workings, these 700 acres (283 hectares) of wetlands are a haven for migrating birds. This nature reserve has been managed by the Royal Society for the Protection of Birds (RSPB) since 1968; a visitor centre and a series of hides have been established to promote public understanding of these birds.

This fantastic walk is great for a full day's outing. As well as the nature reserve this walk also follows footpaths and bridleways through beautiful British farm and woodland. The route goes through the delightful village of Ledsham with one of the oldest Saxon churches in West Yorkshire. Spend a bit of time watching the birds, stop for lunch in Ledsham and then finish with ice creams back at the visitor centre – perfect! Be prepared to squeeze through a number of kissing gates, but it is well worth the effort!

Map: Ordnance Survey 1:25000 Explorer 289 – grid reference 452278

Distance: 5 miles

Getting there: Park in Fairburn Ings RSPB nature reserve car park.

Walk towards the RSPB visitor centre.

There are picnic tables and toilets here as well as ice creams and duck food for sale.

Turn left following the sign to the hides and then take the first left to the Riverbank Trail (keep following the signs for this trail for at least 30 minutes). As you leave the footbridge turn left.

There is a bench here for those that fancy a break already!

Go through a double kiss-
ing gate and turn right.
After a few minutes turn
left through a second kissing gate and go straight
through a third one after 10
minutes.

There are hides all along
the side of the lake for
viewing the wetland birds.

Approximately 30 minutes
into the walk you go
through a wooden barrier
and turn left down a gravel
woodland path towards cut
hide and village facilities.

1. At the end of this track
   go through the kissing
   gate adjoining a metal
   gate straight ahead. This

The Riverbank Trail, Fairburn Ings Nature Reserve

leads you into Well Trough Cottages on Cut Road, Fairburn. Turn
left at the end of this road onto Caudle Hill Road.

Carry along the road passing Ings Mere Court on the left and, just
past a sign for road humps, you will see a 'no through road' on the
right, Beckfield Lane. Go up this lane and after a few minutes take
the right-hand fork. This leads up to a cottage with white gates,
take the path to the right of this.

2. You are now about 1 hour into your walk. Go through the kissing
   gate, then walk along the left edge of the field. You come to a
   second gate next to a wooded area (Caudle Hill Plantation) and go
   through the adjoining kissing gate.

Look behind you for great views over the RSPB nature reserve.

Keep following this footpath through another kissing gate, keep
to the right edge of this field, and along to Wormstall Wood.

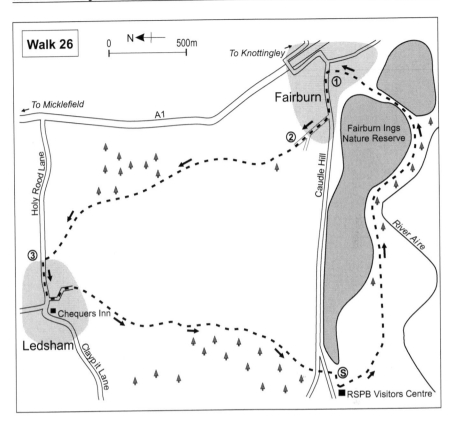

You should be able to see the village of Ledsham to the left.

Half way along the field you pass underneath some telephone cables and the path forks, take the left path towards the middle of the field not the path along the fence. You come to another kissing gate on the edge of the wood and then the path goes left through the wood to a stile. Lift the pushchair over the stile (two people needed here) and go straight across the field to the woodland ahead.

Look out for a stile into the wood on the right. You can just fit the pushchair through the gap at the left of this stile. The path passes along the edge of the wood, drops down a small slope and leads you back to the fields; do not take any paths to the right. Go along the edge of the field, ignore the gateway to the left, and continue straight ahead. Go past a small stile and the path curves round some tall trees towards the village.

3. After 1 hour 45 minutes you will come to a gate with a kissing gate to the left. This takes you onto the main road where you turn left into village of Ledsham. As you go into the village you will see All Saints Church ahead of you. Opposite the church is a 'no through road', Newfield Lane, signposted as a bridleway, so turn left down here to continue the walk.

If you fancy a break and perhaps some food there is a child friendly pub, the Chequers Inn, just a few minutes further along the main road. It has a large beer garden and they are happy to heat up your baby food.

As you go down Newfield Road go left at a fork next to Grange Cottage (don't go down Manor Garth cul-de-sac) and past white gables on your left. This takes you onto a dirt track which leads into a field.

Walk down this track for about 30 mins passing between fields, with many breaks in the hedges, and alongside the edge of some woodland. As you leave the woodland you come to a road and you should be able to see the RSPB centre ahead. Go across the short stretch of field in front of you and then cross over a second road and find your car in the car park.

In the area

If you fancy a bit of shopping for yourself and the kids then pop into **Freeport Castleford Outlet Centre** just off junction 32 of the M62. There are over 65 shops here as well as cafés.

Next door to the outlet centre is **Xscape**, www.xscape.co.uk/castleford or telephone 0871 222 5671, an incredible entertainment centre for the whole family. It has a real snow ski slope, rock and ice climbing walls, an aerial assault course, a multi-screen cinema, bowling lanes, skating, an amusement arcade, a laser zone as well as shops and restaurants all under one roof!

Walk 27: Pugneys Country Park, Wakefield

Allow: *45 minutes*

This is an easy little stroll for a hot summer's day. There are plenty of places to stop for a picnic and you can even take a dip in the lake to cool off! The park opens daily at 9.00am and closes at 9.00pm or sunset. There is a miniature train, Pugneys Light Railway, which runs along the west side of the large lake.

Pugneys Country Park was opened as a nature reserve and water sports park in 1985. The park has been developed on reclaimed land that was once an opencast mine and a sand and gravel quarry. The development started in the 1970s and the 250-acre (101 hectares) site now has two lakes. The large lake is used for water sports and canoes, windsurfers, dinghies and pedaloes are available for hire. The small lake is a nature reserve and the waterfowl can be viewed from two bird hides.

Map: Ordnance Survey 1:25000 Explorer 278 – grid reference 324179

Distance: 1½ miles

Getting there: The park is located just off junction 39 of the M1 on Denby Dale Road (A636). Parking and entry to the park are free. There is a visitor centre with café (with highchairs) and toilets with baby changing facilities at the entrance to the park.

Walk to the far end of the car park with the visitor centre behind you and the large lake on your right-hand side. Go through the gateway and along the white gravel path. There are benches all along the route.

On the top of the hill ahead you will be able to see the ruins of Sandal Castle.

1. After 5 minutes you will come to a T-junction, turn right and then

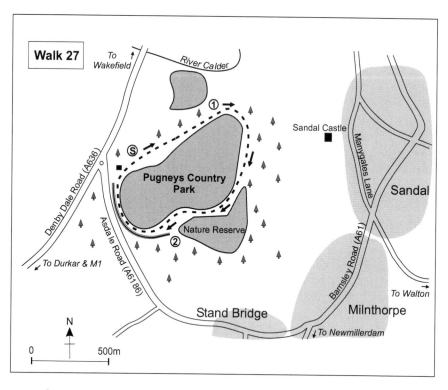

right again at the next junction so that you are continuing to follow the path around the lake.

There is a beach area here where the water is shallow enough for a swim!

As you continue to follow the path around the lake you will see the second smaller lake on the left.

There is a hide on the path where you can get a great vantage point to view the birds within this nature reserve.

2. You will soon see the tracks for Pugneys Light Railway on your left. Continue around the lake towards the visitor centre. There is often an ice-cream van in the car park, so treat yourself before the journey home.

Pugneys Country Park

In the area

Sandal Castle can be seen from the lake and is only a short drive away. This castle dates from the 12th century and overlooks the site of the Battle of Wakefield (1460). The castle was demolished in 1645 but was restored to present condition in the 1970s. Admission is free.

The **National Coal Mining Museum**, Overton, www.ncm.org.uk or telephone 01924 848 806, is open daily 10am - 5pm. Children under 5 aren't allowed underground but they can visit the pit ponies, take a trip on the paddy or loco trains, play in the miners' adventure playground or walk the nature trail. Entry to the museum is free.

Walk 28: Newmillerdam, Wakefield

Allow: 1hr 30mins

This is a lovely, easy walk, which can be extended or shortened along the way. The paths are wide and the tracks take you through wooded areas and alongside the lake, where there are plenty of ducks to feed. There are no refreshment stops, but if you are lucky there is sometimes an ice cream van at the end of the walk. There's also a pub with a beer garden opposite the car park.

The lake at Newmillerdam Country Park was created by damming Bushcliff Beck in about 1285. In 1954, the site was sold to the former Wakefield Corporation as a public amenity.

Map: Ordnance Survey 1:25000 Explorer 278 – grid reference 331157

Distance: 3 miles

Getting there: Park in the car park, for Newmillerdam Country Park, which is on Barnsley Road (A61), opposite the Fox & Hounds pub. This is a pay and display car park, so have some coins handy.

Make your way down to the bottom of the car park and take a right through two black metal bollards, with the lake on your left. In a couple of minutes, you will come to a wooden gate, go through it and just keep to the main path. After about fifteen minutes, you will come to a fork. Take the right-hand path here (which is basically straight on).

1. Soon you will pass over a little stone bridge and a couple of minutes after that you will see a bench straight ahead. Turn right here, following the main path.

   If you want to cut this walk down by twenty minutes, turn left over the bridge here and pick up directions from paragraph marked ***

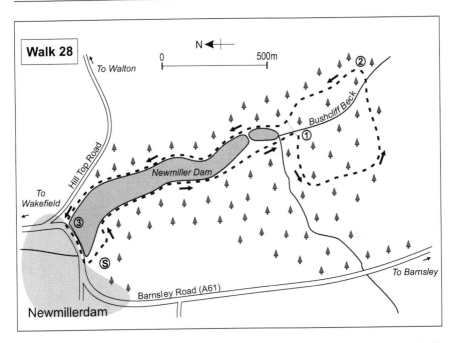

Soon there is another fork in the road where you need to turn left. After another five minutes or so, you come to the end of the track with a bench in front. Turn left here, heading downwards where the path is quite sandy. Keep straight to this path and take the second left-hand turning.

2. In roughly ten minutes, the path forks again. You need to take the left-hand path downwards. Soon the woods open up and you rejoin the main path again, which veers slightly to your right.

*** If you have taken the short cut, cross over the bridge and turn left and follow the directions below.

3. Eventually you will reach some white gates at the end of the path. Go through the gates and turn left onto the pavement, heading back towards the car park. If it's a sunny day, there might even be and ice cream van here.

Footpath causeway, Newmillerdam

In the area

Secker Wood Local Nature Reserve is just off the A61, south of Newmillerdam. It is a site of special scientific interest with a mixture of dry heath, wet heath and semi-woodland, providing a rich habitat for wildlife. For more information, call 01924 303 980.

The Heronry, **Waterton Countryside Discovery Centre and Anglers Country Park** is just off Haw Park Lane (off the A638) – seven miles south-east of Wakefield. There's a picnic area and visitor centre and it's ideal for walking. For more information, call 01924 303 980.

Walk 29: Yorkshire Sculpture Park, Wakefield

Allow: 1 hour 30 minutes

At last, a chance for intellectual stimulation and artistic inspiration whilst you are taking the little one for a walk! The Yorkshire Sculpture Park is a wonderful 500 acre (202 hectare) 18th-century park at the heart of which is Bretton Hall, now part of the University of Leeds. Wander through the grounds and view sculptures by international artists as well as the famous local sculptors Henry Moore (1898-1986), born in Castleford and Barbara Hepworth (1903-1975), who was born in Wakefield .

This walk shows you the full scope of the park, taking you through grassy fields, along farm tracks and through woodland. It does involve lifting the pushchair over one stile, so make sure you don't go alone. There are many other walks to be done within the grounds, some of which are suitable for four wheeled pushchairs.

Map: Ordnance Survey 1:25000 Explorer 278 – grid reference 285132

Distance: 2½ miles

Getting there: Leave your car in the car park and make your way to the entrance of the Yorkshire Sculpture Park visitor centre. There is a parking charge but no entrance fee to the park.

Take the path to the immediate left of the visitor centre. Go down a few steps and then through the gate into the park. The path goes directly down the hill with a woodland area on your right. This is signposted as the dog-walking route. You will pass some picnic tables on the right and a sign to more tables in the woodland area.

Continue down the hill towards the River Dearne passing Henry Moor's sculpture of a seated woman, and crossing over a couple of paths on the way. When you come to the bottom of the hill go

through the gateway on
your right signposted to the
lower park and Cascade
Bridge.

1. The path passes through
   a narrow area of wood-
   land after which there is
   a bridge on your left and
   Bretton Hall on your
   right. Take the path up
   towards Bretton Hall
   and then the next path
   on your left, crossing the
   park below the hall.
   After about 10 mins you
   will come to a gate
   signed to Cascade
   Bridge and Longside
   Gallery. Go through the
   kissing gate and turn
   left.

Sculpture by Henry Moore

2. The path crosses two bridges, one over the river and the second
   over the lake. Immediately after the lake you come to some large
   gates. Go through the gates and follow the path round to the left
   towards Longside Gallery. After the second gate, follow the path
   up the hill, don't go left into the woodland. The path is a dirt track
   with deep ruts and could be very muddy in wet weather.

The track bends to the left in the middle of the field and on your
right you can see the Longside Gallery at the top of the hill. When
the track splits take the right-hand fork and follow the path,
ignoring tracks off to the left.

The path to the left is part of an old racetrack.

At the border of some woodland (Oxley Bank Wood) there is a

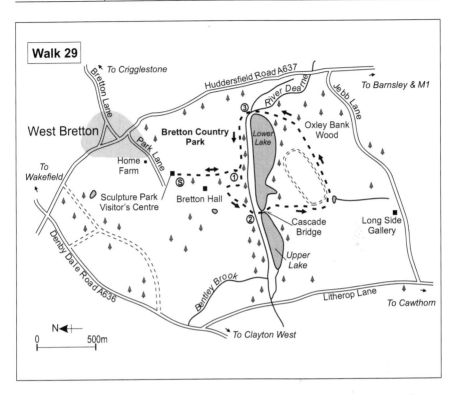

stone wall with a narrow stile. Lift the pushchair over the stile, go down the steps to the left and then up the steps ahead of you.

There is a picnic table here for those who fancy a break before you head back towards the visitor centre.

Follow the path ahead which is signed to the Yorkshire Sculpture Centre. The path heads down through the woodland and down a series of wooden steps. Turn right at the bottom and follow the track round.

3. Go over the bridge with the lake on your left and a series of water cascades to the right. Take the second bridge over the river and go through the gate ahead. Turn left and walk alongside the river. Go through the next gate and eventually you come to the gate to Cascade Bridge (marker 1 on the map). Do not go through this gate

but turn right and head up the hill back to the visitor centre, ignoring all paths to your left and right.

In the area

Kirklees Light Railway (telephone 01484 865 727), has small steam trains running between local towns every weekend of the year and every day between the end of May and beginning of September. It's even possible to combine a ride on the train with a circular walk (see walk 24)!

Magna, the science adventure centre, is just down the road in Sheffield and has a great adventure playground for the under-fives. More details of opening times and special events can be found at www.visitmagna.co.uk or telephone 01709 720 002.

Walk 30: Upton Nature Reserve, Upton

Allow: *2 hours 30 minutes*

Upton Nature Reserve is home to around 150 bird species. There are also many butterflies, dragonflies, some snakes and reportedly lizards! We just saw birds and butterflies on our visit though …

The paths are nice and easy for all-terrain pushchairs, with varied views of lakes, fields and woodland. However, there is a very small section of this walk, which requires crossing over a roundabout to rejoin the path. It is well worth doing though as the lake is lovely at the other side.

It is also worth noting that there are no picnic tables or refreshment stops on this walk, so go stocked up with plenty of your own supplies and a picnic blanket!

Map: Ordnance Survey 1:25000 Explorer 278 – grid reference 477133

Distance: 4½ miles

Getting there: Park near the fishing lake, just off High Street.

When you are organised with the pram etc, come out of the car park and turn left onto High Street. After a couple of minutes, turn left again following the Public Footpath sign going through a kissing gate. The track here is quite narrow.

After a couple of minutes the path forks. Take the right-hand path, then right again in a few yards, to take you over a little stone bridge (this is where the path used to be a railway track). Soon you will pass a pond on the left. The path forks again after a few minutes, and you need to go left here. Then there is another fork, bear left again and keep going.

1. Soon you will get to a steel kissing gate with the main road ahead.

Lake at North Elmsall Common

Go through the gate and turn left on the main road where you will see a roundabout (please be extra careful here as it is quite tricky to get across). The path is on the opposite side of the roundabout, after the second road exit and is signposted for Minsthorpe Lane and the West Yorkshire Cycle Route.

Go through the green kissing gate and head downward. After a while the path opens up on both sides to fields and on a clear day you can see South Elmsall and South Kirkby.

2. After about twenty minutes the track changes colour from black to white. Keep going straight on the white track for about a minute or so until you see a second path joining from the left. Turn left onto this path and follow it downwards. Eventually you will come to a fork in the path, take the right-hand fork and keep to this path all the way round the lake, with the lake on your left-hand side. (Take care here as, after about fifteen minutes, the path veers off straight ahead and you would end up walking through fields – as we nearly did ...). It should take about an hour to get here.

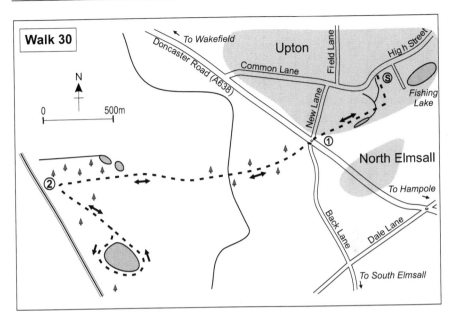

Eventually, the path around the lake brings you back to the main track again. Now it is just a case of heading back to the car. So, follow the track back upwards and when you get to the junction again (with the black and white path), turn right on to the path and keep straight on until you come to the green kissing gate.

Go through the kissing gate and cross over the roundabout (please take extra care here as it is quite tricky to see all the traffic). Turn right just before Bridge House towards the steel kissing gate. Go through the kissing gate and keep to this track until you pass over the stone bridge and come to a fork in the road.

Take the left fork back towards the main road. Eventually you will get to the wooden gate from the start of the walk. Go through this wooden gate and turn right along the main road, then your next right, which will lead you back to the car park.

In the area

Hemsworth Waterpark and Playworld in Kinsley has gardens, lakes with beaches, pedaloes and a miniature railway. Playworld (open school holidays and weekends) is an adventure playground for kids from toddlers to teens. There is also a family-friendly pub, picnic areas and a wildlife zone. The address is Hoyle Mill Road, Kinsley, Near Pontefract, telephone 01977 617 617.

Nostell Priory is a National Trust property that not only has a great house to look round but also lovely lakeside and parkland walks. There is a teashop with baby feeding and changing facilities and a children's play area. If you get bored of pushing the buggy they have slings and children's hip seats for hire! Check out the National Trust website, www.nationaltrust.org.uk, for opening times or ring 01924 863892.